Parenting, Education, and Social Mobility in Rural China

Like many countries around the world, China has been implementing policies aimed at improving parent–school relationships. However, unlike many developed countries, the historical context of family–school relationships has been limited and parents typically do not participate in the school context. Until now, there has been little research conducted in rural China on parental involvement in their children's education.

This book investigates the nature of parental involvement in primary children's education in rural China by using a combination of quantitative and qualitative methods. It outlines the layered strategies of how rural parents are involved in their children's schooling, showing that rural parents strongly desire educational success for their children and view education as a means to their children gaining social mobility. It demonstrates that few rural parents engage in visible forms of parental involvement in their children's schools, such as attending parent–teacher meetings. Rather, they are more likely to engage strategies to support their children's education that are largely invisible to schools. It adds to the growing body of parental involvement research that suggests that culture, location, and socioeconomic status influence different forms of parental involvement and highlights nuances in invisible forms of parental involvement.

Providing insights into how poor rural parents envision their role with their children, schools, and the larger society, and how these relationships can affect the social mobility of students and families, this book will be of huge interest to students and scholars of Asian education, comparative and international education, and Chinese society.

Peggy A. Kong is an assistant professor in Comparative and International Education at Lehigh University, USA. Her Chinese Education research interests include educational inequality including rural education, gender issues, and private tutoring.

Routledge Contemporary China Series

1 **Nationalism, Democracy and National Integration in China**
Leong Liew and Wang Shaoguang

2 **Hong Kong's Tortuous Democratization**
A comparative analysis
Ming Sing

3 **China's Business Reforms**
Institutional challenges in a globalised economy
Edited by Russell Smyth, On Kit Tam, Malcolm Warner and Cherrie Zhu

4 **Challenges for China's Development**
An enterprise perspective
Edited by David H. Brown and Alasdair MacBean

5 **New Crime in China**
Public order and human rights
Ron Keith and Zhiqiu Lin

6 **Non-Governmental Organizations in Contemporary China**
Paving the way to civil society?
Qiusha Ma

7 **Globalization and the Chinese City**
Fulong Wu

8 **The Politics of China's Accession to the World Trade Organization**
The dragon goes global
Hui Feng

9 **Narrating China**
Jia Pingwa and his fictional world
Yiyan Wang

10 **Sex, Science and Morality in China**
Joanne McMillan

11 **Politics in China Since 1949**
Legitimizing authoritarian rule
Robert Weatherley

12 **International Human Resource Management in Chinese Multinationals**
Jie Shen and Vincent Edwards

13 **Unemployment in China**
Economy, human resources and labour markets
Edited by Grace Lee and Malcolm Warner

14 **China and Africa**
Engagement and compromise
Ian Taylor

15 **Gender and Education in China**
Gender discourses and women's schooling in the early twentieth century
Paul J. Bailey

16 **SARS**
Reception and interpretation in three Chinese cities
Edited by Deborah Davis and Helen Siu

17 **Human Security and the Chinese State**
Historical transformations and the modern quest for sovereignty
Robert E. Bedeski

18 **Gender and Work in Urban China**
Women workers of the unlucky generation
Liu Jieyu

19 **China's State Enterprise Reform**
From Marx to the market
John Hassard, Jackie Sheehan, Meixiang Zhou, Jane Terpstra-Tong and Jonathan Morris

20 **Cultural Heritage Management in China**
Preserving the cities of the Pearl River Delta
Edited by Hilary du Cros and Yok-shiu F. Lee

21 **Paying for Progress**
Public finance, human welfare and inequality in china
Edited by Vivienne Shue and Christine Wong

22 **China's Foreign Trade Policy**
The new constituencies
Edited by Ka Zeng

23 **Hong Kong, China**
Learning to belong to a nation
Gordon Mathews, Tai-lok Lui, and Eric Kit-wai Ma

24 **China Turns to Multilateralism**
Foreign policy and regional security
Edited by Guoguang Wu and Helen Lansdowne

25 **Tourism and Tibetan Culture in Transition**
A place called Shangrila
Åshild Kolås

26 **China's Emerging Cities**
The making of new urbanism
Edited by Fulong Wu

27 **China-US Relations Transformed**
Perceptions and strategic interactions
Edited by Suisheng Zhao

28 **The Chinese Party-State in the 21st Century**
Adaptation and the reinvention of legitimacy
Edited by André Laliberté and Marc Lanteigne

29 **Political Change in Macao**
Sonny Shiu-Hing Lo

30 **China's Energy Geopolitics**
The Shanghai Cooperation Organization and Central Asia
Thrassy N. Marketos

31 **Regime Legitimacy in Contemporary China**
Institutional change and stability
Edited by Thomas Heberer and Gunter Schubert

32 **U.S.-China Relations**
China policy on Capitol Hill
Tao Xie

33 **Chinese Kinship**
Contemporary anthropological perspectives
Edited by Susanne Brandtstädter and Gonçalo D. Santos

34 **Politics and Government in Hong Kong**
Crisis under Chinese sovereignty
Edited by Ming Sing

35 **Rethinking Chinese Popular Culture**
Cannibalizations of the canon
Edited by Carlos Rojas and Eileen Cheng-yin Chow

36 **Institutional Balancing in the Asia Pacific**
Economic interdependence and China's rise
Kai He

37 **Rent Seeking in China**
Edited by Tak-Wing Ngo and Yongping Wu

38 **China, Xinjiang and Central Asia**
History, transition and crossborder interaction into the 21st century
Edited by Colin Mackerras and Michael Clarke

39 **Intellectual Property Rights in China**
Politics of piracy, trade and protection
Gordon Cheung

40 **Developing China**
Land, politics and social conditions
George C.S. Lin

41 **State and Society Responses to Social Welfare Needs in China**
Serving the people
Edited by Jonathan Schwartz and Shawn Shieh

42 **Gay and Lesbian Subculture in Urban China**
Loretta Wing Wah Ho

43 **The Politics of Heritage Tourism in China**
A view from Lijiang
Xiaobo Su and Peggy Teo

44 **Suicide and Justice**
A Chinese perspective
Wu Fei

45 **Management Training and Development in China**
Educating managers in a globalized economy
Edited by Malcolm Warner and Keith Goodall

46 **Patron-Client Politics and Elections in Hong Kong**
Bruce Kam-kwan Kwong

47 **Chinese Family Business and the Equal Inheritance System**
Unravelling the myth
Victor Zheng

48 **Reconciling State, Market and Civil Society in China**
The long march towards prosperity
Paolo Urio

49 **Innovation in China**
The Chinese software industry
Shang-Ling Jui

50 **Mobility, Migration and the Chinese Scientific Research System**
Koen Jonkers

51 **Chinese Film Stars**
Edited by Mary Farquhar and Yingjin Zhang

52 **Chinese Male Homosexualities**
Memba, Tongzhi and Golden Boy
Travis S.K. Kong

53 **Industrialisation and Rural Livelihoods in China**
Agricultural processing in Sichuan
Susanne Lingohr-Wolf

54 **Law, Policy and Practice on China's Periphery**
Selective adaptation and institutional capacity
Pitman B. Potter

55 **China-Africa Development Relations**
Edited by Christopher M. Dent

56 **Neoliberalism and Culture in China and Hong Kong**
The countdown of time
Hai Ren

57 **China's Higher Education Reform and Internationalisation**
Edited by Janette Ryan

58 **Law, Wealth and Power in China**
Commercial law reforms in context
Edited by John Garrick

59 **Religion in Contemporary China**
Revitalization and innovation
Edited by Adam Yuet Chau

60 **Consumer-Citizens of China**
The role of foreign brands in the imagined future china
Kelly Tian and Lily Dong

61 **The Chinese Communist Party and China's Capitalist Revolution**
The political impact of the market
Lance L. P. Gore

62 **China's Homeless Generation**
Voices from the veterans of the Chinese civil war, 1940s–1990s
Joshua Fan

63 **In Search of China's Development Model**
Beyond the Beijing consensus
Edited by S. Philip Hsu, Suisheng Zhao and Yu-Shan Wu

64 **Xinjiang and China's Rise in Central Asia, 1949–2009**
A history
Michael E. Clarke

65 **Trade Unions in China**
The challenge of labour unrest
Tim Pringle

66 **China's Changing Workplace**
Dynamism, diversity and disparity
Edited by Peter Sheldon, Sunghoon Kim, Yiqiong Li and Malcolm Warner

67 **Leisure and Power in Urban China**
Everyday life in a medium-sized Chinese city
Unn Målfrid H. Rolandsen

68 **China, Oil and Global Politics**
Philip Andrews-Speed and Roland Dannreuther

69 **Education Reform in China**
Edited by Janette Ryan

70 **Social Policy and Migration in China**
Lida Fan

71 **China's One Child Policy and Multiple Caregiving**
Raising little Suns in Xiamen
Esther C. L. Goh

72 **Politics and Markets in Rural China**
Edited by Björn Alpermann

73 **China's New Underclass**
Paid domestic labour
Xinying Hu

74 **Poverty and Development in China**
Alternative approaches to poverty assessment
Lu Caizhen

75 **International Governance and Regimes**
A Chinese perspective
Peter Kien-Hong Yu

76 **HIV/AIDS in China – The Economic and Social Determinants**
Dylan Sutherland and Jennifer Y. J. Hsu

77 **Looking for Work in Post-Socialist China**
Governance, active job seekers and the new Chinese labor market
Feng Xu

78 **Sino-Latin American Relations**
Edited by K.C. Fung and Alicia Garcia-Herrero

79 **Mao's China and the Sino-Soviet Split**
Ideological dilemma
Mingjiang Li

80 **Law and Policy for China's Market Socialism**
Edited by John Garrick

81 **China-Taiwan Relations in a Global Context**
Taiwan's foreign policy and relations
Edited by C. X. George Wei

82 **The Chinese Transformation of Corporate Culture**
Colin S.C. Hawes

83 **Mapping Media in China**
Region, province, locality
Edited by Wanning Sun and Jenny Chio

84 **China, the West and the Myth of New Public Management**
Neoliberalism and its discontents
Paolo Urio

85 **The Lahu Minority in Southwest China**
A response to ethnic marginalization on the frontier
Jianxiong Ma

86 **Social Capital and Institutional Constraints**
A comparative analysis of China, Taiwan and the US
Joonmo Son

87 **Southern China**
Industry, development and industrial policy
Marco R. Di Tommaso, Lauretta Rubini and Elisa Barbieri

88 **State-Market Interactions in China's Reform Era**
Local state competition and global market building in the tobacco industry
Junmin Wang

89 **The Reception and Rendition of Freud in China**
China's Freudian slip
Edited by Tao Jiang and Philip J. Ivanhoe

90 **Sinologism**
An alternative to Orientalism and Postcolonialism
Ming Dong Gu

91 **The Middle Class in Neoliberal China**
Governing risk, life-building, and themed spaces
Hai Ren

92 **The Chinese Corporatist State**
Adaption, survival and resistance
Edited by Jennifer Y.J. Hsu and Reza Hasmath

93 **Law and Fair Work in China**
Sean Cooney, Sarah Biddulph and Ying Zhu

94 **Guangdong and Chinese Diaspora**
The changing landscape of Qiaoxiang
Yow Cheun Hoe

95 **The Shanghai Alleyway House**
A vanishing urban vernacular
Gregory Bracken

96 **Chinese Globalization**
A profile of people-based global connections in China
Jiaming Sun and Scott Lancaster

97 **Disruptive Innovation in Chinese and Indian Businesses**
The strategic implications for local entrepreneurs and global incumbents
Peter Ping Li

98 **Corporate Governance and Banking in China**
Michael Tan

99 **Gender, Modernity and Male Migrant Workers in China**
Becoming a 'modern' man
Xiaodong Lin

100 **Emissions, Pollutants and Environmental Policy in China**
Designing a national emissions trading system
Bo Miao

101 **Sustainable Development in China**
Edited by Curtis Andressen, Mubarak A.R. and Xiaoyi Wang

102 **Islam and China's Hong Kong**
Ethnic identity, Muslim networks and the new Silk Road
Wai-Yip Ho

103 **International Regimes in China**
Domestic implementation of the international fisheries agreements
Gianluca Ferraro

104 **Rural Migrants in Urban China**
Enclaves and transient urbanism
Fulong Wu, Fangzhu Zhang and Chris Webster

105 **State-Led Privatization in China**
The politics of economic reform
Jin Zeng

106 **China's Supreme Court**
Ronald C. Keith, Zhiqiu Lin and Shumei Hou

107 **Queer Sinophone Cultures**
Howard Chiang and Ari Larissa Heinrich

108 **New Confucianism in Twenty-First Century China**
The construction of a discourse
Jesús Solé-Farràs

109 **Christian Values in Communist China**
Gerda Wielander

110 **China and Global Trade Governance**
China's first decade in the World Trade Organization
Edited by Ka Zeng and Wei Liang

111 **The China Model and Global Political Economy**
Comparison, impact, and interaction
Ming Wan

112 **Chinese Middle Classes**
China, Taiwan, Macao and Hong Kong
Edited by Hsin-Huang Michael Hsiao

113 **Economy Hotels in China**
A glocalized innovative hospitality sector
Songshan Sam Huang and Xuhua Michael Sun

114 **The Uyghur Lobby**
Global networks, coalitions and strategies of the World Uyghur Congress
Yu-Wen Chen

115 **Housing Inequality in Chinese Cities**
Edited by Youqin Huang and Si-ming Li

116 **Transforming Chinese Cities**
Edited by Mark Y. Wang, Pookong Kee and Jia Gao

117 **Popular Media, Social Emotion and Public Discourse in Contemporary China**
Shuyu Kong

118 **Globalization and Public Sector Reform in China**
Kjeld Erik Brødsgaard

119 **Religion and Ecological Sustainability in China**
Edited by James Miller, Dan Smyer Yu and Peter van der Veer

120 **Comparatizing Taiwan**
Edited by Shu-mei Shih and Ping-hui Liao

121 **Entertaining the Nation**
Chinese television in the twenty-first century
Edited by Ruoyun Bai and Geng Song

122 **Local Governance Innovation in China**
Experimentation, diffusion, and defiance
Edited by Jessica C. Teets and William Hurst

123 **Footbinding and Women's Labor in Sichuan**
Hill Gates

124 **Incentives for Innovation in China**
Building an innovative economy
Xuedong Ding and Jun Li

125 **Conflict and Cooperation in Sino-US Relations**
Change and continuity, causes and cures
Edited by Jean-Marc F. Blanchard and Simon Shen

126 **Chinese Environmental Aesthetics**
Wangheng Chen, translated by Feng Su, edited by Gerald Cipriani

127 **China's Military Procurement in the Reform Era**
The setting of new directions
Yoram Evron

128 **Forecasting China's Future**
Dominance or collapse?
Roger Irvine

129 **Chinese Migration and Economic Relations with Europe**
Edited by Marco Sanfilippo and Agnieszka Weinar

130 **Party Hegemony and Entrepreneurial Power in China**
Institutional change in the film and music industries
Elena Meyer-Clement

131 **Explaining Railway Reform in China**
A train of property rights re-arrangements
Linda Tjia Yin-nor

132 **Irony, Cynicism and the Chinese State**
Edited by Hans Steinmüller and Susanne Brandtstädter

133 **Animation in China**
History, aesthetics, media
Sean Macdonald

134 **Parenting, Education, and Social Mobility in Rural China**
Cultivating dragons and phoenixes
Peggy A. Kong

135 **Disability Policy in China**
Child and family experiences
Xiaoyuan Shang and Karen R. Fisher

136 **The Politics of Controlling Organized Crime in Greater China**
Sonny Shiu-Hing Lo

137 **Inside Xinjiang**
Space, place and power in
China's Muslim far northwest
*Edited by Anna Hayes
and Michael Clarke*

138 **China's Strategic Priorities**
*Edited by Jonathan H. Ping
and Brett McCormick*

Parenting, Education, and Social Mobility in Rural China

Cultivating dragons and phoenixes

Peggy A. Kong

LONDON AND NEW YORK

First published 2016
by Routledge
2 Park Square, Milton Park, Abingdon, Oxon OX14 4RN

and by Routledge
711 Third Avenue, New York, NY 10017

Routledge is an imprint of the Taylor & Francis Group, an informa business

© 2016 Peggy A. Kong

The right of Peggy A. Kong to be identified as author of this work has been asserted by her in accordance with sections 77 and 78 of the Copyright, Designs and Patents Act 1988.

All rights reserved. No part of this book may be reprinted or reproduced or utilised in any form or by any electronic, mechanical, or other means, now known or hereafter invented, including photocopying and recording, or in any information storage or retrieval system, without permission in writing from the publishers.

Trademark notice: Product or corporate names may be trademarks or registered trademarks, and are used only for identification and explanation without intent to infringe.

British Library Cataloguing in Publication Data
A catalogue record for this book is available from the British Library

Library of Congress Cataloging-in-Publication Data
Kong, Peggy A.
  Parenting, education and social mobility in rural China : cultivating dragons and phoenixes / Peggy A. Kong.
    pages cm — (Routledge contemporary China series ; 134)
  Includes bibliographical references and index.
  1. Rural youth—Education—China. 2. Home and school—China.
  3. Educational sociology—China. I. Title.
  LC5148.C6K66 2015
  370.9173′40951—dc23
  2015021301

ISBN: 978-1-138-84820-7 (hbk)
ISBN: 978-1-315-72616-8 (ebk)

Typeset in Times New Roman
by Apex CoVantage, LLC

Printed and bound in Great Britain by
TJ International Ltd, Padstow, Cornwall

Contents

List of figures		xiv
List of tables		xv
Acknowledgements		xvi
	Introduction	1
1	Parental involvement and social class in China: conceptual and theoretical framework	11
2	What it means to be "rural"	27
3	Parental hopes and desires	47
4	Student's role in their own success	62
5	Active rural parents' hidden work: creating a good learning environment	75
6	Information network: support of family and friends	91
7	Migration for education	103
	Conclusion	115
Bibliography		123
Index		129

Figures

I.1	Gansu Province, GSCF counties marked	4
1.1	Conceptual framework for rural parental involvement	25
2.1	School gate	36
2.2	Desks and students	37
3.1	Mother's educational aspirations in 2000 and 2004 by child's sex	49
3.2	Courtyard	53
3.3	House	54
3.4	*Kang*	56
3.5	Farm plot	58
3.6	Mother's educational aspirations and child achievement (2000)	59
3.7	Mother's educational aspirations and child achievement (2004)	60
6.1	Pig	95

Tables

1.1	Descriptive statistics of Zhengxing County primary schools	6
2.1	Summary of family background statistics	30
2.2	Basic family background descriptives	31
5.1	Summary statistics for selected variables	88
5.2	Parental educational expectations and child chore status	89
5.3	Parameter estimates (and standard errors and p values) for a taxonomy of logistic regression models for parental educational expectations and child chore status, controlling for background characteristics	89

Acknowledgements

This research project has been an adventure that has allowed me to enter the lives of so many amazing people. I do not think I will ever be able to express my gratitude for all the love, support, guidance, and patience that I have been shown throughout the years. The experiences and relationships that have developed over the years have enriched my life forever. First and foremost, this research would not be possible without the collaboration of the rural parents, teachers, administrators, and children who were willing to share their lives with me. I want to thank the wonderful parents, teachers, administrators, and children in this study. I feel honored by their generosity and humbled as they welcomed me into their homes and never expected anything in return. The community in Zhengxing warmly embraced my presence and ensured that I was safe, well-fed, and experienced life in rural Gansu. In return for their openness, support, and trust in this research, I have tried to faithfully portray the lives of all the participants in my study. I want to recognize that without the generous support of the David Boren Fellowship, Harvard University Frederick Sheldon Traveling Grant, Hong Kong Research Grants Council, General Research Fund-HKU 746010H, and Harvard University Center for International Development Traveling Grant, the extensive travel and data collection would not have been possible. In addition, the Gansu Survey of Children of Families (GSCF) was generously funded by The United Kingdom Economic and Social Research Council. Deparment for International Development (ESRC/DfID) Joint Scheme for research on International Poverty Reduction, the World Bank, the Spencer Foundation, and the United States National Institutes of Health.

This research started out at the Harvard School of Education (HGSE), where many faculty and students provided valuable input into the design, data collection, and analysis. I want to thank HGSE faculty for guiding and mentoring my research interests, including Eleanor Drago-Severson, Vanessa Fong, Suzanne Grant Lewis, and John B. Willett. I benefited tremendously from friends who generously spent time listening to my ideas, reading drafts, and coding interview transcript data. I want to thank Shaher Banu Vagh, Sandra Huang, Adriana Katzew, Anju Saigal, Nancy Sharkey, Tere Sorde-Marti, and Peichi Tung-Waite for their support and friendship over the years.

This research project grew out of my work with the Gansu Survey of Children and Families team. Working on this project has deepened my appreciation for interdisciplinary work as well as my passion for rural education in China. Thank you Jenifer Adams, Paul Glewwe, Emily Hannum, Xiaodong Liu, Chunping Lu, Albert Park, Tanja Sargent, Yanhong Zhang, Yuping Zhang, and Mingren Zhao. Their support and knowledge of Chinese education and society have been instrumental in my research projects. I want to thank Emily for providing critical and supportive feedback and Jennifer for lively discussions about logistic regression, family life, and rural education. I am grateful to Tanja for nudging me to tell the story and always encouraging me with "*jiayou.*" Yuping has always been a great sounding board for my rambling thoughts and provided companionship during writing.

I have been fortunate to be surrounded by amazing colleagues at Lehigh University and at the University of Hong Kong who have encouraged and nurtured this book. My program faculty including Sothy Eng, Iveta Silova, and Alexander Wiseman, along with our wonderful graduate students provided a stimulating intellectual environment for this project. While at the University of Hong Kong, my department chair, Gerard Postiglione, supported this research and motivated many other research projects. I really appreciate the hours upon hours Gerry spent with me in his office discussing the changing dynamics of rural life, families, and education in China. I am also especially thankful to Kai-ming Cheng, Gregory Fairbrother, and Dan Wang, for sharing their knowledge of China, fieldwork experience in China, and Chinese education with me over the years. I want to thank Greg for reading numerous drafts and providing candid and critical feedback.

Stephanie Rogers and Rebecca Lawrence at Routledge Press provided sustained support and encouragement of this project. I appreciate the careful reading by two anonymous reviewers. The anonymous reviewers provided helpful feedback and I have tried to incorporate many of their suggestions. Three chapters in this book draw from previously published research. I want to thank National University of Singapore Press (NUS Press) for permission to reuse of material from Kong (2010), "To walk out": Rural Parents' Views on Education. *China: An International Journal*, 8(2), 360–373. Copyright 2010.

This research has benefited from the support and love of friends and family. Over the years, Niclas Ericsson, Colleen Mahar-Piersma, and Nancy Yim encouraged and provided intellectual and social balance to my life. To Dajiujiu, Zhou Guofei, Zhou Guocheng, Xiaofeng Jie, Jiefu, Zhou Yinxiang, and Zhou Yanshan for all your support during fieldwork. Thank you for navigating me through local cultural dynamics and sharing wonderful meals together. I am thankful for having the continued support of Mary, Brian, Steve Mulvaney and Anne Baker. My brother and his family, Peter, Michelle, Audrey, Olivia, Sabine, and Calder Kong for reminding me to eat well and laugh a little! Peter thank you for always keeping me grounded and asking the most penetrating questions.

I want to thank my parents, Ngai and Tsai-chih Kong, who taught me the importance of education, and taking that step to migrate for better educational opportunities. I am eternally grateful to my mother for her wisdom, strength, humor, patience, and love. Without my mother, I would not have been able to conduct this research. My 100 year-old grandmother, Kuo-Fen Tan, who fought to attend school for the first time when she was eleven years old inspires me every single day with her kindness, perseverance, and thirst for knowledge. Michael Mulvaney, thank you for being my friend and partner in life. Your unwavering support of my career included reading drafts of this project and caring for our children during my absences. Jack and Madeleine, thank you for sharing with me all the books you wrote while I was writing this book. I dedicate this book to my grandmother, my parents, and all the parents in my study. Their hard work and perseverance, step-by-step has taught me about family support and encouraged this book.

Introduction

On two exploratory trips to rural areas in Gansu, I spoke with mothers and fathers about the role of parents in their children's schooling, and parents responded enthusiastically with both excitement and exasperation, "I want to help my child and support their education, but I don't know how"[1] and "I send my child to school, I don't know what else to do to help them."[2] Parents all wanted to support their child's education but felt that did not know how to do so. In one breath, rural parents said they wanted to do something but at the same time they didn't know what to do. In our conversations, parents explained to me that they felt limited because they themselves had never been to school or had limited experience with formal schooling. To me this showed that parents have agency and support their children's education.

Prior to these initial trips, I had spoken with education officials, teachers, and administrators who all told me that rural "parents are all the same, they do not have *wenhua* (the work are uneducated), are busy, don't really *zhongshi* (value) schooling for their children" and even blamed rural parents for not knowing how to help their children and putting all the responsibility for their children's education onto the schools. Many of the concerns mentioned by school officials and education leaders echoed much of the research in developed country contexts about the limited involvement of poor and uneducated parents in their children's schooling. These divergent perspectives between what I was hearing and observing spurred my interest in understanding what parents with both limited schooling experience and resources were doing to support their children's schooling. I was unconvinced by the explanation that rural parents did not care and this sparked my interest in trying to figure out how and what rural parents were doing to support their children's schooling. This study is focused on understanding how poor rural parents in China describe their involvement in their children's schooling and on contextualizing their participation. The objective is not to measure rural parental involvement by current models of involvement, but to provide a more nuanced and reconceptualized understanding of parental involvement in rural China.

Instead of trying to tell parents how to be involved in their children's education, I asked them how they were involved in, participated in, and supported their children's schooling. Throughout my study, parents questioned and were a little skeptical about why my research study focused on rural parents because they were poor and not highly educated. Even as I developed a growing relationship with each family, parents would tell me that I was educated and should tell them the answers to educational success. Parents eagerly wanted to learn how to best to be involved and support their children's schooling. As an outsider to rural China, having grown up in the United States my entire life (with trips to Asia), I would share with parents my educational experiences across different levels of education but emphasized to parents that their educational experience of growing up in rural China and parenting children was very valuable information. Also, I wanted to understand what rural parents are doing instead of trying to offer them solutions, which I was not qualified to do. But, parents would still emphasize that my educational degrees qualified me to by an expert. Mrs. Hong's statement to me that "if this is helpful to you, I, as an uneducated person, can help you [an educated person], then okay" effectively encapsulates rural parental attitudes toward the value of their knowledge. I highly valued the knowledge the rural parents shared with me.

Ethnically, I am Han and look like any other member of the community. Although I looked like a local everyone in the community knew that I was not a local member. However, I was able to listen in on conversations in the schools, in the streets, and on buses and learn about the concerns of rural parents. Linguistically, I was an outsider and parents in my study would tell me that my Mandarin was better than their Mandarin, and proper, like on television, and that they only spoke *tuhua* (dialect). I grew up speaking Mandarin in the home, and on previous research trips to Gansu I learned to understand the local dialect but could not speak it fluently. Parents in my study were also very curious about funding sources for my research trip and job prospects. Having someone else, an organization, fund my research to study them, rural parents, was difficult for my study participants to understand. They asked how someone else could pay for my trip and asked if I was working for a specific company or department. The combination of my being a student and having the funds to travel abroad was bordering on incomprehensible for rural parents in my study. We would discuss the price of international airplane tickets and also travel costs associated for travel within China. Although I was an outsider, families accepted me into their homes and began protecting me as one of their family members.[3]

My role as an outsider – as being a non-rural resident, person pursing a doctorate, and from outside of China – was publicly described by a local principal during a local education meeting. As he spoke he held his right hand flat and level with his forehead and placed his left hand flat near his abdomen, and said that his right hand is *Jiang boshi*'s[4] level, and his left hand was the local area level, and that I had gone through many levels to arrive in Zhengxing. He started by saying that I was working on a doctorate, and slowly moved his right hand downward toward his left hand – saying I had a graduate degree, then a bachelor's degree, then that I was coming from the United States to China, and with each description he moved his right hand down half an inch. I landed in Beijing, flew to Lanzhou, and then took a bus to the township, and then another bus to the local area, and at each level he would explain that I passed through many economic and social levels to arrive in our Zhengxing.

I was also an outsider not only in the physical sense of rural China, but also because I was not a parent when I conducted the study. Parents were very generous in sharing their perspectives, welcoming me into their homes and into the fields as we discussed both their educational experiences and their children's schooling. They allowed me to observe them discipline their children, weep in distress, laugh in happiness, and struggle with their own lack of ability. I listened to what parents had to say and watched their involvement in their children's schooling. In my role as a researcher, my experiences may have influenced how I collected and interpreted the data (Maxwell, 1996), but I implemented several checks to ensure the descriptive, interpretative, and theoretical validity of my work (Maxwell, 1996; Miles & Huberman, 1994). I collected and analyzed data from parents, teachers, and education policy documents.

The fieldwork

To understand parental involvement in their rural children's schooling, I conducted roughly 10 months of fieldwork in China. My fieldwork was focused in the homes of parents, fields, local shops, schools, and local community. It was important for me to participate in all the areas that parents interact to support their children's education. Ethnographic data for this book were collected as part of a field study of parental involvement in children's schooling in a rural community in Gansu province between 2003 and 2005. The study combined participant observation and in-depth interviews with 33 families of sixth-grade students, five teachers, one principal, one district education leader, and one county education bureau leader, with an analysis of policy documents, student essays, and survey data from the Gansu Survey of Children and Families (GSCF). For this book, 15 families are presented to illustrate rural parental involvement in their children's schooling.

Research site

I conducted my research in Gansu province, located in the northwestern part of China and encompassing 390,000 square kilometers of mountains and plateaus. The population of Gansu, according to the 2000 census, is 25.62 million people, with 6.15 million of them living in urban areas and 19.47 million living in rural areas. Gansu was an appropriate site for addressing my research questions because it was one of the poorest provinces in China, with high levels of illiteracy, and I had prior professional and personal connections in the area. I selected Junxi county and Zhengxing township for my research for personal, professional, and substantive reasons.

First, I had family that lived a few hours from my research site. Second, I was familiar with the school district in Junxi and had visited it several times as part of working on the Gansu Survey of Children and Families, a longitudinal interdisciplinary research project investigating the health and well-being of rural children in 20 survey counties in Gansu (see Figure I.1). Lastly, I had a professional relationship with a county education bureau official (forged during my exploratory study in 2003). Junxi was known in the surrounding counties for its diverse population and its high levels of parental participation in schooling. I selected Zhengxing township as my research site based on discussions with Mr. Lu,

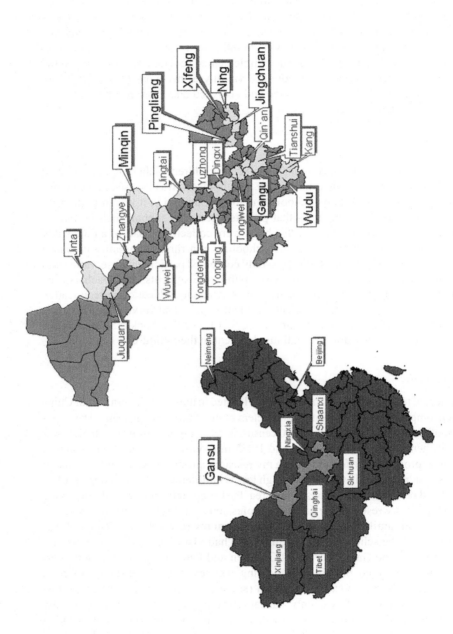

Figure 1.1 Gansu Province, GSCF counties marked
Reprinted with permission from E. Hannum. It has appeared in Hannum, Kong, & Zhang (2009).

the education bureau official, and local teachers. When I first talked to Mr. Lu, the education bureau leader in Junxi county (the county in which Heping City is situated) about my interest in investigating parental involvement in their children's education in rural Junxi, his eyes lit up and he told me that parental involvement and participation in children's schooling was very important. He described to me how the triangular relationship between the home, school, and the community impacted a child's development. He shared with me several youth and education policies and parent education initiatives aimed at promoting improved relationships between the home and school.

Mr. Zhan, the education district leader, and Mr. Xie, the primary school principal, explained to me that in 2002, as part of economic development, the status of Zhengxing was changed from that of a village to a township. In 2003 there were eight villages in Zhengxing, but by 2004 there were only six villages, as two villages had consolidated. Mr. Zhan and Mr. Xie told me that the population of Zhengxing township is roughly 7,800 people. About 2,000 people from surrounding areas also come to the area to work or have businesses there, bringing the total population in the area to just under 10,000.[5] Zhengxing is the seat of the township government.

As you enter Zhengxing there is a beautiful red arch that welcomes you, and when you leave that same arch wishes you well. I looked forward to seeing this arch every time I took the bus out to my field site. The same road that brought me into Zhengxing is the same road that parents wanted their children to use to leave the rural areas. The main road that winds through Zhengxing was one of the main roads that connected western Gansu with the capital, Lanzhou. Up until about 2003, there was heavy truck traffic through Zhengxing, transporting goods and materials to western parts of Gansu. As a result, many families opened up restaurants and shops selling truck parts, snacks, and other sundries along the half-mile of road that runs through Zhengxing. There were 40 to 50 businesses along this small strip of road; however, recent railroad improvements and construction have decreased the amount of road traffic through Zhengxing, and this has resulted in declining economic prosperity. Now, there are only about half as many shops and restaurants along the main strip. I see the road as a metaphor for expectations that parents had for their children – they wanted their children to "exit" and go into the cities, to take the road away from where they were born.

Selection of school and participants

To begin with, I visited all the complete primary schools in Zhengxing township. Table I.1 shows basic information for the primary schools in the area. After discussions with school principals and with Mr. Lu about my research, housing opportunities, and needs of the school, I decided upon Zhengxing Central Primary School.[6] I selected Zhengxing Central Primary School because it had the most diverse student population in the township. Additionally, to optimize data collection, I lived at the Zhengxing Middle School in the teacher dormitories. Zhengxing Central Primary School was the closest primary school to my living quarters. Zhengxing Central Primary School was centrally located along the main public

6 *Introduction*

Table I.1 Descriptive statistics of Zhengxing County primary schools

Name of school	Number of students	Grades	Number of teachers	Number of students in the 6th grade
Lutushui Primary School	20	Pre-K–4	2	N/A
Zhengxing Primary School	420	Pre-K–6	23 18 women 5 men	75
Shaozhu Primary School	155	Pre-K–6	8 5 women 3 men	30
Sagao Primary School	122	Pre-K–6		29
Li Jiachao Primary School	112	Pre-K–6	7 4 women 3 men	15
Bodu Primary School	45	Pre-K–3	3	N/A
Daqi Primary School	100	Pre-K–6	6 3 women 3 men	23
Reqicun	30	Pre-K–4		N/A
Total	1,004			

Source: Mr. Xie and Mr. Zhan (10/14/2004) and school records (11/2/2004).

road and within two kilometers of 15 villages, and the remaining four villages were within 10 kilometers. To reach the outlying villages, I traveled by foot and bicycle.

Zhengxing Central Primary School had 420 students and offered kindergarten through sixth grades. There were 23 teachers in the school, including 18 women and 5 men. There were a total of 13 classes, with two classes per grade, except for kindergarten, which had one. Each class had a *banzhuren* (班主任) who typically taught one of the core courses (Chinese or mathematics) and stayed with the same class from first grade through sixth grade. There were two sixth-grade classrooms, Class 1 and Class 2, with a total of 75 students.[7]

In Class 1, Ms. Li, the *banzhuren* and Chinese teacher, had been with the class since second grade. There were 38 students in Class 1, including 18 girls and 20 boys. However, Ms. Li needed to take a leave of absence during the Spring 2005 semester to study for the teacher credentialing examination. Ms. Li was a *minban* (民办) teacher, meaning she was considered an unofficial teacher. Ms. Shao, the Chinese teacher, took her place as the *banzhuren* of Class 1.

In Class 2, Ms. Gu, the Chinese teacher, had just been announced as the *banzhuren* for the academic year 2004–2005. She was recently transferred to the school from another part of the county. There has been a different banzhuren each year since second grade. The class size was 37, with 18 girls and 19 boys.

I identified participants from the two sixth-grade classrooms for my study using purposive sampling (Patton, 1990). I selected sixth-grade parents for several reasons. First, parental involvement levels are more intense in the primary school when children are younger than in the upper grades. Second, sixth grade is the last grade of primary school, and student dropout rates increase after primary school. I wanted to talk with a range of parents, including those whose children may drop out after primary school. Third, I wanted to interview children to triangulate my data, and I learned while in the field that older children, like fifth and sixth-grade students, were more willing and capable of expressing their feelings than children in younger grades. In selecting these sixth-grade children, I tried to cover the heterogeneity present in the population in terms of family background, home–school interactions, and student achievement levels in order to be able to describe diverse variations and common patterns (Miles & Huberman, 1994). My purpose was not to be representative of the population but to describe diverse experiences.

After observing students in class, I met with the *banzhuren* of each classroom to review student records and discuss student family backgrounds and teacher interactions with parents. After my observations and discussions with the teacher, I selected 16 students (9 girls and 7 boys) from the Class 1 and 17 students (7 girls and 10 boys) from the Class 2 to follow up. I selected students with a range of academic achievement, family economic/education backgrounds, and varying levels of parent–teacher interactions, as described by the *banzhuren*. The participation of the children and their families was completely voluntary. I interviewed the principal of Zhengxing Central Primary School, sixth-grade mathematics, Chinese, and English teachers,[8] parents of selected students, and the selected students themselves.

Theoretical framework

To understand how rural parents describe their involvement in their children's schooling, I draw on Bourdieu's concepts of habitus, field, capital, and social reproduction. These concepts capture the complexity of the lives of rural parents and how they are involved in their children's schooling. The first chapter lays out the theoretical framework and Chapters 2 through 4 illustrate how social and economic changes as well as the lived experiences of rural parents shape their habitus, or dispositions and social position. Habitus allows us to understand rural parents' dispositions of being a rural peasant and how their social position shapes their support for their children's schooling. Bourdieu's concept of habitus and field enables us to capture the agency rural parents engage to support their children's education. Instead of ascribing the discourse of peasant and quality *suzhi* on rural parents, we see how rural parents themselves view the social world they live in— the field in Bourdieu's work. This book seeks to disrupt common conceptions of a peasant in rural China as well as conceptual frameworks for how rural families are involved in their children's schooling.

By focusing specifically on rural parental involvement, we see the invisible forms of support that parents engage to cultivate a good learning environments for their children. Also, the study highlights that poor rural families are doing a lot, they are informed, educating themselves, and acting on the information they have to improve the learning conditions for their children. Parental involvement is not simply a long list of activities that parents must complete. My study finds that rural parents have a clear understanding of the social system, as seen by their own experiences with schools and in society-at-large. Rural parents see that the structures and environments in rural areas are not as good as those in urban areas. Instead of focusing their efforts on changing the system, parents focus their energy on cultivating a strategy that provides their children good academic environments. This book shows that rural parents in the study disrupt the discourse on "peasant" and "backward" as well as the parental involvement literature of rural parents by being active, educated, and strategic for their children's education.

Much of the parental involvement discourse is set up to compare urban and rural parents, especially based in developed country contexts. The research indicates that there are differences in parental involvement, based on socioeconomic differences and the ways that parents engage with schools. However, this research primarily focuses on comparing the different types of parental involvement based on Western concepts of parental involvement. This book expands our understanding of parental involvement to include what I call invisible forms of parental involvement. These are invisible because they are currently not discussed in the parental involvement literature and are invisible to teachers. In this book, the discourse of development, peasant comparison to urban *hukou,* all shape the way rural parents are actively involved in their children's schooling.

Outline of the book

This book is organized into eight chapters. Chapter 1 lays out the theoretical and conceptual framework. Chapter 2 shows how rural residents view the social structures and their role in their children's education. This chapter serves two purposes: first, too often, the voices of poor rural residents are not heard, and their views and behaviors are often ascribed to them. The meaning of being an urban or a rural resident is intimately tied to the Chinese government's *hukou* (household registration) system. Rural parents describe the barriers and opportunities available to *huo* (to live) in China, understanding the rapid social and economic changes in China that impact their lives as rural residents. Second, rural parents detail what being rural means for their children's future in a rapidly changing Chinese environment and how this context frames parent support for education.

Chapter 3 builds on Chapter 2 and moves into rural parental hopes and educational expectations for their children as well as a discussion of education as a means for social mobility for their children. This chapter grounds the book in the ways rural parents approach participation in their children's schooling, specifically holding high educational aspirations. Rural parents seek a non-rural life for their children and want them "to walk out" of the village. Chapter 4 focuses on the role of the student responsibility in their own learning as a critical component of parental involvement in their children's schooling. Students are overlooked in the discussion of parental participation. Recent government policies focus on youth and highlight the important role that youth themselves play in their education and development. Researchers in developed country contexts have found that poor and less educated parents often place responsibility for their children's success in school on teachers and students themselves. Rural parents in my study resonate with previous work; rural parents feel that educational success is "up to them [their children]" and that their children are responsible for their own success in school. This point of view was consistent across educated and less-educated parents in the study. Rural parents are in a precarious position because of their own limited educational experiences. They feel they play a marginal role in their children's education, and their participation includes conceptualizing their children as being responsible for their own learning. This chapter highlights what it means for children to be responsible for their own learning through parent and student voices.

Chapter 5 offers a glimpse into the provision of a good learning environment as an invisible form of parental involvement. Much of the parental support and participation of poor families are often overlooked, as poor families are busy working to support their families, in both developed and developing countries. Few rural parents engaged in visible forms of parental involvement in their children's schools, such as attending parent–teacher meetings, school events, or parent–teacher associations. This chapter captures the work that rural parents do engage in to support their children's education including additional paid work, housework, and unpaid work to allow children to focus on their schooling.

Chapter 6 discusses the kinship and non-kinship networks that poor families draw on to support their children's schooling. In developed country contexts, researchers have found differences in the types of kinship and non-kinship patterns of wealthy and less wealthy families, with wealthier families having more kinship and non-kinship ties with school personnel. This chapter identifies the kinship and non-kinship ties that rural parents engage to support their children's schooling. Rural parents have extensive kinship and non-kinship ties with school personnel and are more comfortable with these ties than formal parent–teacher relationships to support their children's schooling. Understanding how parents view social and kinship ties in supporting their children's education is key to securing information and support for children's schooling.

Chapter 7 details how rural parents strategize and plan for migration in search of educational opportunities for their children. In the developed country context, the phenomenon of middle-class families migrating to better schooling districts to improve the educational options for their children is well-known. I find that rural parents in China also use this strategy to support their children's schooling. This is very impressive in the rural Chinese context, given the *hukou* system. Migration in China is highly regulated, and permanent or formal change of residence requires approval by local authorities. In addition to the household registration system, it takes a large amount of resources and planning to move from one rural area to another or even to a township. Beyond resources, migration means moving away from familial and social supports. Poor rural residents with little education are making the move for their children.

10 *Introduction*

The final chapter concludes with a discussion of how schools, families, and communities work together. In the Chinese context, the three pillars of support for children's schooling are schools, families, and society. Chinese society has been rapidly developing, which shapes how poor families actively support their children's schooling but also offers opportunity for parents to participate in their children's schooling. This book presents how rural parents conceptualize parental participation in their children's schooling that includes children taking responsibility for their learning, holding high educational expectations, engaging material resources to help children navigate the school space, working multiple jobs, and migrating to support their children's schooling. Rural parents work toward social mobility through improved educational opportunities for their children. This chapter closes by offering suggestions for improving parent–school relations to support children's schooling.

Notes

1 Juhua Township mother's comment that was often repeated by other parents
2 Junxi Village mother's statement that was echoed by many parents
3 On more than one occasion while I was in a family's home while parishioners of local temples visited the house soliciting donations for repairs or travel support; merchants would enter the home to sell their wares. Both parishioners and merchants would ask each adult in the room for funds or interest in purchasing goods. As the parishioner or merchant would approach me, before I had a chance to respond, parents in my study would start waving their hands in the parishioner or merchant's face and say that I was a family member and not interested in donating or purchasing wares. Parishioners and merchants are persistent, and while at Qi Youkang's house, Qi Youkang's mother physically stood up, with her legs slightly bent, and bobbed on the balls of her feet as she spread her arms as to defend me from a parishioner.
4 My family name in Mandarin is Jiang, but in the Cantonese dialect it is Kong. As my father is Cantonese, my last name was translated to Kong when he immigrated to the United States. *Boshi* is a title signifying one that has a doctorate.
5 According to 2006 data from Junxi County, there are 11,067 residents in Zhengxing.
6 I wanted to study the parents of 6th graders and therefore only visited complete primary schools. Incomplete primary schools accepted children for kindergarten through fourth grade.
7 Referred to as Class1 and Class2.
8 This included the homeroom teacher of each class.

1 Parental involvement and social class in China

Conceptual and theoretical framework

In this book, rural parental involvement in children's education is my phenomenon of interest. In this chapter, I first briefly review the literature on parental involvement, then situate the study within cultural and social reproduction. Next, I describe China's modernization, including the discourse on *suzhi* and peasants in China, then outline recent educational reforms and conclude the chapter with a description of the conceptual framework for the book, describing the mechanism of how rural parents strategize their involvement in their children's schooling. A gap currently exists in the parental involvement literature in non-Western-country contexts and about how parents with little educational experiences and wealth are involved in their children's schooling. The focus of the book is, How do rural parents define their involvement in their children's schooling? What shapes their support for their children's schooling? What strategies do they implement to support their children's schooling?

Studies in Western-country contexts suggest that based on family background, wealthier and more educated families have more resources and provide more support for their children's education. Similarly, based on family social class, there are differences in the types of interactions that parents have with teachers and school personnel, with ensuing consequences for the child's education (Lareau, 1987; Reay, 1998). Finally, the forms of interactions that parents have with other parents in the school also differ by social class. These interactions have been shown to impact children's education (Lareau, 1987, 2000; Reay, 1998).

Parental involvement

Parental willingness and ability to help their children's education are important because research has shown that when parents are involved in schools more fully, their children tend to enjoy greater educational success (Buchmann, 2002; Ho & Willms, 1996; McNeal, 1999; Schneider & Coleman, 1993; Zellman & Waterman, 1998). However, despite growing evidence that parental support and involvement are linked to positive schooling outcomes, there have been few rigorous and comprehensive studies that have explored parental perceptions and practices about their children's education. Most studies have investigated parental involvement as a predictor of student achievement, and few have actually examined how parents describe their own involvement (see Mapp, 2003; Smrekar & Cohen-Vogel, 2001; and Pena, 2001, for exceptions).

Previous research has depicted parental involvement in terms of helping their children with their homework, attending school events, communicating with teachers, reading to children in the home, and providing a learning environment in the home (Lee & Bowen, 2006). I separate these forms of parental involvement into visible and invisible forms that benefit children's schooling. From the teacher's perspective, attendance at school events and communicating with teachers are considered visible forms of parental involvement, while helping children with homework and providing a home learning environment are invisible forms of parental involvement. In my study, I demonstrate that poor rural parents in Gansu engage in invisible forms of parental involvement, such as sacrificing parents' time and energy to work extra jobs and do housework, establishing social relationships to support their children's schooling, and migrating with their families to better academic environments.

What do visible forms of parental involvement in their children's education look like?

Programs and policies that support parental involvement in schooling have focused mainly on improving what I call the visible forms of parental involvement.[1] Parents are encouraged to attend school events, parent–teacher meetings, observe in classrooms, and communicate with teachers. In short, parents are visible to the school and to the teacher. Visible forms of parental involvement to teachers and schools take two main forms: (a) interactions between parents and school personnel, including teachers and principals, and (b) parental participation in school-sponsored activities (Carbonaro, 1998; Goyette & Conchas, 2001; Ho & Willms, 1996; Lareau, 1987; Reay, 1998; Kalmijn & Kraaykamp, 1996). In their study of the impact of parental involvement on eighth-grade student achievement in the U.S., Ho and Willms (1996) found that parental involvement as school volunteers or at parent–teacher organization (PTO) meetings had little influence on student achievement. Joyce Epstein's (2001) pioneering work in the area of parent, school, and community partnerships offers a six-component framework that includes parenting, communicating, learning at home, decision making, volunteering, and collaboration with the community.

The second form of parental involvement in schooling is invisible parental involvement. I characterize invisible forms of parental involvement as (a) parental provision of a constructive home learning environment for the child, (b) parental aspirations for their children, (c) direct parent–child interactions, (d) parental regulation of the child's schedule, and (e) parental knowledge of their child's friends' parents. In their quantitative study of social capital in home and school environments in the U.S., Parcel and Dufur (2001) cite the importance of parental provision of a constructive learning environment in the home and include in their analyses indicators of the provision of educational supplies to the child, including a dictionary, desk, and academic materials. Other quantitative studies conducted in the U.S. conclude that home supervision, including parental regulation/monitoring of a child's schedule, are associated with positive schooling outcomes for the child (Goyette & Conchas, 2001; Ho & Willms, 1996; McNeal, 1999). Finally, other researchers have found strong relationships between the presence of constructive parent–child interactions – such as parents helping their children with homework and talking with them about academic interests – and ultimate student achievement (Coleman, 1988; McNeal, 1999; Parcel & Dufur, 2001). Intergenerational closure is also a form of parental involvement that is not visible to teachers, which Carbonaro (1998)[2] defines as an individual-level trait that reflects the relationship between a parent and their children's friends' parents. Carbonaro (1998) conducted a study on the impact of intergenerational closure on educational outcomes. He measured intergenerational closure by asking about parent knowledge of a child's friends' parents and found that higher levels of intergenerational closure were positively associated with mathematics achievement but not with achievement in reading, history, or science.

Differences between visible and invisible forms of parental involvement – race, ethnicity, and social class

There is a growing body of research showing that different forms of parental involvement are invisible to schools, and this book intends to extend this research. Studies focused on parental involvement as a predictor of achievement find that middle-class parents are more involved and volunteer in schools (Desimone, 1999) and are proactive in the schooling context (Horvat, Weininger, & Lareau (2003). Also, parenting practices vary based on socioeconomic status (Hill & Taylor, 2004). A U.S. quantitative study by Lee and Bowen (2006) focused on five types of parental involvement in their children's education and included both visible and invisible forms of involvement. Lee and Bowen (2006) found that poverty and race consistently predicted student academic achievement. All of the parents in their study appeared interested in their children's schooling, but the types of involvement in which they engaged differed based on their racial, economic, and educational backgrounds (Lee & Bowen, 2006). A key finding was that European American parents, wealthier parents, and more educated parents were more present in their children's schools, and that teachers may interpret a lack of visible parental involvement in schools as a sign that the parents lack interest in their children's schooling. Lee and Bowen (2006) suggest that this may then disadvantage non-European children, children from poorer homes, and children from less-educated families, whose parents are less visible in the school. They suggest that future educational policies and programs should consider the many ways that parents are involved in schooling and not only the ways that schools would like the parents to be involved.

Parents drew upon social and community support as a form of invisible parental involvement. In a study that investigated parental involvement of Chinese American and African American parents in their children's schooling, both African American and Chinese American parents participated in invisible forms of parental involvement (Diamond, Ling & Gomez, 2004). However, African American parents were more comfortable raising educational concerns with their children's teachers and schools. Chinese Americans, on the other hand, deferred to the teacher as the educational expert and preferred to provide behind-the-scenes support, such as provision of supplementary learning resources (Diamond, Ling, & Gomez, 2004). Both groups drew on community-based support in the form of social networks to provide time, money, educational resources, and educational information to support their children's schooling (Diamond, Ling, & Gomez, 2004). Diamond, Ling, and Gomez (2004) suggested that future studies must examine other less visible forms of parental involvement, such as community-based support for schooling. Chao's (1996, 2000) work comparing Chinese and European immigrants revealed that Chinese immigrant mothers played an active role in helping with homework and believed in the process of hard work. Pena's (2001) study of Mexican American parents also emphasized the importance of social networks that advantage some parents and prevent others from being involved in their children's schooling. Pena suggests that teachers need to tap into these social networks to improve the information flow between themselves and the parents. Most of the literature on parental involvement has been developed in Western country and urban contexts with little research in developing country contexts.[3]

Conceptions of parental involvement in China

There have been few studies conducted in China that focus specifically on parental involvement. The few studies that discuss parental involvement in children's schooling in the Chinese context focus on the kinds of parental involvement that are considered invisible forms of parental involvement. In addition, most research on Chinese family involvement in children's education has focused on research settings in urban China and has research settings in urban China and few studies have been conducted in rural areas.

A more complete understanding of the cultural, financial, and historical context of the lives of rural parents can shed light on the ways that rural parents in China support their children's schooling. Culturally, rural and urban areas are alike in that we see in both places a division between the expected role of parents and teachers in children's schooling, and this division shapes the role that parents play in their children's schooling. Rural parents are less wealthy than urban parents, and their financial circumstances shape the type of support they offer their children. However, rural and urban areas are different in terms of the unequal school resources and quality and also the official designation or residents as urban or rural, which will be discussed later in the chapter. Linguistically, *Putonghua* is the language of instruction in schools. However, there are eight or nine main dialects across the country and in rural areas *Putonghua* is not spoken, except in schools. In rural Gansu, each area has their own local dialect, and those from outside of Gansu often have trouble understanding the dialects. Historically, state-sanctioned parental involvement has been limited, and rural parents had limited involvement in their children's schooling.[4]

In the Chinese context, Chinese parents prefer to participate in invisible forms of parental involvement in their children's schooling. Stevenson and Stigler (1992) summarize the historical and cultural reasons why parental involvement in their children's education may differ between China and the U.S. Based on a study conducted in Beijing, these scholars assert that Chinese parents and teachers work together to support children's education by adopting non-overlapping, but complementary, roles. They suggest that parents see their roles as helpers in the home, by checking their children's homework, providing them with a supportive home learning environment, and communicating with teachers via a daily diary. They found that few parents attended parent–teacher meetings because they did not understand the importance of these meetings. A study by Chi & Rao (2003) about rural parental beliefs about schooling and their children's academic achievement found that parents turned over responsibility of schooling to the children's teachers. Rural parents viewed teachers as the person primarily responsible for their children's academic learning and limited their own role to paying school fees. A recent book by Andrew Kipnis (2011a) analyzes educational desire for education for both urban and rural residents within the context of China's political and cultural context.

In the urban Chinese context, researchers have investigated the impact of parental involvement on the mathematics achievement of children in Beijing (Stevenson, Lee, & Stigler, 1986), and Vanessa Fong's study (2004) of urban Chinese youth, enrolled in secondary school and above, found that parents were willing to work several jobs, endanger their own health, forgo meals and comfortable living spaces, and take on household chores to support their children's education. Urban Dalian parents support the idea that their children will not be like them; they want a better life for them and are willing to continue to support their children with additional education in order that they will attain an appropriate position in the workplace. They enable their children's attitude of not settling for any position but settling for one that is appropriate with their education.

There are few studies of parental involvement in rural China, but there is evidence that rural parents do indeed support their children's education. In her description of rural family life in China, Jing Lin (1993) noted that rural parents were willing to support their children's education but that rural children were disadvantaged compared to urban students. Lin portrayed rural children, during the Mao era and during China's economic reform, as having fewer financial resources, limited parental academic help, and less time to study than their urban counterparts (Lin, 1993). Family incomes in rural families were lower than in urban families and rural parents had difficulty coaching or helping their children with homework because of their own limited education (Lin, 1993). In contrast, parents in wealthier urban areas were willing to forfeit their life's savings to pay a child's school tuition, to wear simpler and cheaper clothes, and to spend their free time coaching their children (Lin, 1993). Additionally, rural children had taken on additional household chores, which lessened the time they spent on academic studies (Lin, 1993). Lin (1993) suggested that the development of a market-oriented economy had shown rural farmers the importance of knowledge and skills, but at the same time, rural parents needed the additional labor of their children on the farm. Moreover, Lin indicated that when rural parents saw the difficult realities that rural children faced in the education system, they withdrew them from school. One study of parental education and student achievement in rural China (Brown, 2002) found that more-educated families have more education-related goods in their homes for their children. In my earlier work in rural Gansu, I also found that differences in family wealth accounted for differences in parental investment support in their children's schooling (Kong, 2003).

Social reproduction and cultural capital

To understand how rural parents support their children's education, I situate my work within Bourdieu's work on social and cultural reproduction and cultural capital. Typically, Bourdieu's (1977a) work on social and cultural reproduction offers a rationale for why children from families with fewer resources are disadvantaged. Bourdieu theorizes that parents with little cultural capital are limited in their ability to support their children's schooling (Bourdieu, 1977a). In addition, Bourdieu (1977a) states that rural parents have had little experience with the education system (cultural capital) and, therefore, are not able to provide their children with the tools to benefit from the education system. In this study I examine the concepts of habitus, field, and capital to understand how rural parents are involved in their children's education, if they have limited understanding of the schooling structures, and then how their own educational experiences, social location, and discourse of their class shape their involvement in their children's schooling.

In describing the cultural and social reproduction functions of schools, Bourdieu (1977a, p. 494) explains that knowledge of the dominant culture is central to success in an education system, so that training can be "received and acquired only by subjects endowed with the system of predispositions that is the condition for the success of the transmission and of the inculcation of the culture." Therefore, children from backgrounds where parents are unfamiliar with the dominant culture, such as those in a "lower position, occupied by the agricultural professions, workers, and small tradespeople" do not have the disposition to receive and acquire training from the education system (Bourdieu, 1977a, p. 488). He explains that the education system anticipates that everyone will be familiar with the dominant culture, but that the education system does not itself offer understanding of the dominant culture.

Capital

Bourdieu (1990), working within the French context, posited that the social world contains several forms of capital: (a) economic capital, in the form of monetary assets; (b) cultural capital, including linguistic and cultural competencies; and

(c) social capital, in the form of resources drawn from social networks and group memberships. The most powerful form of capital is symbolic capital, which is the form that other capitals take when they achieve legitimacy. Bourdieu (1984, p. 114) argues that social classes are differentiated by the "the overall volume of capital, understood as the set of actually usable resources and powers—economic capital, cultural capital, and social capital." Bourdieu (1984) views the various forms of capital as interchangeable and posits that the distribution of economic, social, and cultural capital varies by social class.

Habitus and field

Two critical concepts in Bourdieu's work are habitus and field. In his discussion of class condition and social conditioning, Bourdieu (1984) presents the formula "[(habitus) × (capital)] + field = practice" (p.101). Bourdieu (1990) described habitus "as a system of acquired dispositions." Bourdieu (1977b) believed that the word disposition was best-suited to describe the concept of habitus because disposition not only conveyed something like structure, but also predispositions (a way of being). Habitus is then both a system for producing practices as well as a way of perceiving and appreciating practices (Bourdieu, 1990). Bourdieu (1990, p. 131–132) described habitus as expressing

> the social position in which it was constructed . . . Thus, the habitus implies a "sense of one's place" but also a "sense of the other's place" . . . Firstly, it presupposes that taste (or habitus) as a system of classifactory models is objectively referred, via the social conditionings which produced it, to a social condition: agents classify themselves, expose themselves to classification, by choosing, in conformity with their tastes . . . which go well together and which they also find agreeable or, more exactly, which they find suitable for their position.

A person's habitus is shaped by the structures around them as well as their own past experiences, typically in the early years of life. In this study, rural parental education and their parental perceptions shape their practices to support their children's education.

Field is defined as the structures within which we interact, including society and schools where practice occurs. Field allows for habitus to be dynamic:

> The relation between habitus and field operates in two ways. On one side, it is a relation of conditioning: the field structures the habitus, which is the embodiment of the immanent necessity of the field (or of a hierarchy of intersecting fields). On the one side, it is a relation of knowledge or cognitive construction: habitus contributes to constituting the field as a meaningful world, a world endowed with sense or with value, in which it is worth investing one's energy.
>
> (Bourdieu, in Wacquant, 1989, 44)

Reay (2004) suggests that an exciting way to look at the concepts of habitus, capital, and field is to consider the agency involved in these interactions. In contrast to the notion that one's habitus is fixed and leads to deterministic practice, Reay (2004) suggests that "habitus becomes active in relation to a field, and the same habitus can lead to very different practices and stances depending on the state of the field" (p. 432). Habitus is not fixed and is developed through socialization in the early years in the home and then is redeveloped with interactions in different fields, such as school, work, and family life. An example of when habitus and field are aligned:

> Social reality exists, so to speak twice, in things and in mind, in fields and in habitus, outside and inside social agents. And when habitus encounters a social world of which it is the product, it is like a "fish in water": it does feel the weight of the water and it takes the world about itself for granted.
> (Bourdieu & Wacquant, 1992, p.127)

Sayer's (2005) work on habitus and social class suggests that a perfect alignment between habitus and field may not exist. Sayer (2005) echoes Reay's point (2004) that habitus is activated or not activated is dependent on the context. Sayer (2005) gives the example of

> when we are in a familiar context, these dispositions give us a "feel for the game," an ability to cope and go on effectively without conscious deliberation and planning. In such conditions, the workings of the habitus tend not to be noticed; its influence is clearer when we experience the discomfort of finding ourselves out of place, in an unfamiliar social setting, in which we *lack* a feel for the game.
> (p. 25)

As a result, individuals may do well when they are familiar with the situation and rules of the game but also may flounder when in unfamiliar circumstances. Reay (2004) proposes that at the core of Bourdieu's concept of habitus is choice. And choices are made when habitus and field interact. By examining both habitus and field we can better understand rural parents' dispositions, but also how rural parents respond to the field and new social conditions, such as how they are involved in their children's schooling.

Parental involvement as social and cultural capital

Parents' involvement in their children's schooling has often been conceptualized as a form of social and cultural capital, as mentioned earlier. Annette Lareau (1987) and Diane Reay (1998) have operationalized cultural capital in their work on families and schools. Lareau (1987) posits that Bourdieu's concept of cultural capital needs to be activated in order to create social advantage. Lareau (1987) found that the social and cultural capital in working-class families is valuable but is not consistent with the expectations of the school. Diane Reay's (1998) study of mothers' involvement in their children's schooling found that working-class mothers had difficulty acting expertly with their children's teachers and that teachers held different expectations of parental involvement based on social class.

Annette Lareau (1987, 2000) used Bourdieu's concept of cultural capital to clarify the social processes that occur within the home–school relationship. She engaged Bourdieu's concept of cultural capital and posited that cultural capital needs to be activated in order to have social advantage. Thus, she modified Bourdieu's passive conception and insisted that activity underlay cultural capital. Lareau (1987) used qualitative methods to study parental involvement in two first-grade classrooms in the United States. She suggested that wealthier families tended to align their social and cultural capital with the expectations of the school. She also found that middle-class mothers spent considerable time talking with each other, learning and sharing information about their children's academic development. She described this relationship as being interconnected. In contrast, working-class mothers did not have the same pattern of involvement and referred to their interactions as ones of separateness. Surprisingly, Lareau found that both working-class and middle-class parents equally valued educational success for their children. She also found that it was in the interactions between parents and schools that yielded different teacher responses. Lareau suggested that the social and cultural capital in working-class families is valuable, but not consistent with the expectations of the school, thus indicating that working-class families do not have the tools to benefit from the schooling environment.

Diane Reay's research adds further complexity to the connections between social class and education. Different from Lareau, Reay (1998) asserted that cultural capital exists in all interactions between the home and school, and that the relationship between the two is more complicated than the social marker of middle-class or working-class. Reay's (1998) qualitative study of mothers' involvement in their children's schooling in two neighborhoods in London found that both working-class and middle-class mothers actively supported their fifth-grade children's schooling. Reay's working-class mothers did not have lower levels of involvement with teachers than did middle-class mothers but did engage in less effective educational practices. Working-class mothers were poorly equipped financially, socially, and psychologically to interact expertly with their children's teachers. They found it difficult to assume the role of educational expert, and they were less likely to persuade teachers to address their complaints. Middle-class mothers, in contrast, exhibited confidence, self-belief and self-presentation and were often effective in convincing teachers to accept their points of view (Reay, 1998). Finally, in contrast to Lareau (2000), who found that teachers made similar requests for involvement from both working-class and middle-class mothers, Reay (1998) found that teachers have different expectations for parental involvement based on social class.

Both Reay (1998) and Lareau (2000) have deepened our understanding of parental involvement in how cultural capital serves to advantage middle-class families as they help their children negotiate the school space. Drawing on Bourdieu's work, both Reay and Lareau demonstrate how middle-class families know the rules of school success and more effectively activate and align the home resources, attitudes, and behaviors with the expectations of the school. In the Chinese context, the concept of *suzhi* (quality) similarly exists to explain not only how individuals possess *suzhi*, which allows them to be successful, but is also used to define individuals and a class of society as lacking *suzhi*. In China, instead of addressing the social inequities of society, urban residents are viewed as deserving their educational successes because they have high *suzhi*, while rural peasants have been described as backward and lacking *suzhi*,. In the next section, I outline the concept of *suzhi* for China's modernization and include a discussion of rural peasants.

Suzhi *and education for China's modernization*

In the post-Mao era, two terms, *suzhi* and *wenming*, have been important for spurring China's development (Jacka, Kipnis, & Sargeson, 2013). Kipnis (2011a, 2011b), Greenhalgh (2010), and Murphy (2004b) have highlighted the use of *renkou suzhi* (population quality) to motivate China's development into a modern nation, with modern citizens. The discourse of China's current modernization and development over the last 30 years posits the need to prepare China for global competition. China's policy discourse has focused on modernization and the notion that in order to achieve a modern society, China must educate the people in its backward rural areas. In addition to laying the groundwork for decentralizing China's education system, The Decision on the Reform of the Education Structure of 1985 outlined China's current educational development with a focus on modernizing China:

> Compulsory education is national education which all school-age children and youths receive by law and which the state, community and families are required to support. Being essential to production and to modern life, such education is a hallmark of modern civilization. China's elementary education is still backward. This is in sharp conflict with the people's urgent demand for building a prosperous and powerful socialist country which is highly democratic and civilized.
>
> (1985, "Decision," Section 2)

The importance of education for China's modernization was reaffirmed in June 1999, in The Decision on the Deepening of Educational Reform and the Full Promotion of Quality Education. China's President Hu Jintao emphasized the importance of addressing disparities between urban and rural areas in his report to the Seventeenth National Congress of the Communist Party of China on October 15, 2007. Again, in a government White Paper (2007) titled *The Aid-the-Rural-Poor*

Program in the Early Period of the 21st Century, rural areas were highlighted as both the successes and challenges to relieving poverty in China. The government perspective is that most Chinese have enough to eat and wear, but rural backwardness still remains and poses a challenge to China's development (White Paper, 2007). The government still needs to improve the "quality of life and comprehensive quality of the poverty-stricken people"(White Paper, 2007). In short, rural residents are viewed as culturally backward, and their development is important to China's overall development. To prepare China for global competition, the government acknowledges two important components. First, China needs to improve and upgrade the *suzhi* of the Chinese people. Second, those that are viewed as lacking *suzhi* are rural peasants (Murphy, 2004a).

Even prior to China's current strides toward modernization that advantage urban centers, rural areas have been cast as backwards and lacking. *Suzhi* is a cultural term that rationalizes the social hierarchy in China. At a collective level, nations and groups are can be ordered based on their level of *suzhi*. On an individual level, it is readily accepted that some people have higher *suzhi* intellect, ability, and therefore deserve success. On the other hand, those that have low *suzhi* are seen as not capable and poor quality, and lacking. In her study investigating the use of *suzhi* in turning rural peasants into modern Chinese citizens, Rachel Murphy (2004a, p. 5) posited that the "*suzhi* discourse also serves to maintain state legitimacy because it deflects attention from inequalities arising from policy biases by explaining socio-economic position of individuals in terms of their *suzhi*."

Suzhi, *peasant, and civilization*

Kipnis (2011a) suggests that *suzhi* has long been associated with notions of social class, and the slur that a person lacks "quality" is often directed against "peasants" or other "uncultured" people. *Wenming* (civilization) is used to discuss a more civilized society that does not spit in public places, litter, or use foul language. In rural contexts, peasants are portrayed and ideologically created as backward people who must undergo civilizing (Cohen, 1993; Kelliher, 1994). Kipnis (1997) highlights the change in 1978, after Zhao Ziyang's speech to the Thirteenth Party Congress that returned the conceptions of peasants back to being *luohuo* (backward). Zhao Ziyang stated that

> the primary stage of socialism is the stage for gradually casting off poverty and backwardness; it is the stage of gradually replacing a country where farming based on manual labor farmers the basis and peasants constitute the majority, with a modern industrial nation where nonpeasant workers constitute the majority (Zhao 1989; 10–11).
>
> (As cited in Kipnis, 1997, p. 168–169)

To address the components of improving the *suzhi* of Chinese citizens and rural peasants as having low *suzhi*, education has been critical to improving the overall national strength *suzhi* of the Chinese people (Dello-Iacova, 2009). Emerging in the 1990s and 2000s, the language of *suzhi* emerged in educational reform discourse. Educational reforms focused on "education for quality" (*suzhi jiaoyu*). Part of this focus on "education for quality" is a result of human quality campaigns as a result of the birth-control policy, to encourage a reduction in the number of children so that quality citizens could be supported. These educational reforms enhanced creativity, child-centered learning, and also more military training and political indoctrination (Kipnis, 2011a), placing the onus of improving one's social position in society on the individual.

Interestingly, Murphy (2004a) found that rural parents accepted their lowly place in the world and incorporated *suzhi* discourse into their daily lives but felt empowered to change the direction of *suzhi* discourse. Kipnis (2011b) suggests the contradictory ideas of governing in terms of subjectification and *suzhi* discourse. The idea is that *suzhi* will raise individual autonomy in political discourse while at the same time, in China, serving to ensure commitment to the Chinese regime. The intertwined social, political, educational, and economic structures in China serve as the fields in which rural parents interact and shape the habitus of rural parents. This includes the discourse on the meaning of a peasant, *suzhi* (educational quality), and modernizing China. Based on their interactions with the fields of society and education, rural parents have internalized their class conditions; this, too, affects their view of society and schools. It is important to understand that rural parents' social designation is legally and formally tied to their *hukou*, household registration, and essentially ascribing low *suzhi* to rural parents.

The hukou *system and reform*

Stratification in Chinese society stems largely from the rights citizens enjoy based on their *hukou*, household registration. *Hukou* was introduced in the 1950s as a tool for migration control (Fan, 2008). Every Chinese citizen has a *hukou* location based on his or her residence as a defining marker of household designation. Residents were categorized into agricultural (rural) and non-agricultural (urban). Rural residents included those registered and residing in villages and townships, and urban residents included those registered and residing in larger towns and cities. One's *hukou* status is inherited from one's parents. Rights and access to resources are tied to one's *hukou*. Rural residents have access to farmland while urban residents have access to urban jobs, housing, food, and state-sponsored benefits. As a result, the *hukou* system serves to dictate one's social location and position in society. At the same time, the *hukou* system clearly labels who is considered local and who is not local (Jacka, Kipnis, & Sargeson, 2013). Prior to the mid-1980s, it was difficult for rural residents to migrate to urban areas because food, housing, and jobs were allocated by the state. As China has been modernizing, the division between resources and entitlements based on one's *hukou* status has grown.

Since the mid-1980s, China has implemented several major changes to the *hukou* system that allow for more migration of rural residents. These reforms began with temporary migration residence permits that allowed rural residents to temporarily live in urban areas. Along with these reforms, the marketization of food and housing gave rural residents access to housing and food while in urban areas. A recent study by Hao, Hu, and Lo (2014) of the *hukou* system and educational stratification in China found that "individuals with rural *hukou* assigned at birth are more likely to follow the lowest educational trajectory than their urban-*hukou* counterparts, which could be offset by childhood *hukou* change, a small-probability event" (p. 532).[5]

Chinese educational context

As an element of recent market reforms, the Chinese education system has undergone drastic changes designed to improve its quality and efficiency. The 1980s and 1990s brought radical decentralization to the education system. Educational finance reform was a key component of *The Decision on the Reform of the Education Structure of 1985,* including legislation that gradually transferred the responsibility for the generation and distribution of education funding from the central government to local communities (Tsang, 1994). A year later, the Chinese government enacted the *Compulsory Education Law of 1986,* which provided for nine years of free compulsory education for all children. However, as a result of this law, schools were empowered to charge miscellaneous fees to cover the increased costs of these new provisions. Thus, decentralization has tightened the link between the strength of a local community's economy and the quality of the schools available to its children (Cheng, 1996). Increased local autonomy in administration and access to new sources of educational finance have increased the quality of education available to many in China but have raised concerns about the growing disparities in access (Tsui, 1997; Wei, Tsang, Xu, & Chen, 1999). The introduction of educational fees has disadvantaged children in rural communities who are least able to subsidize schools (Davis, 1989; Lewin, 1994). Hannum and Park (2002) found that, in Gansu in 2000, roughly 70 percent of daily operating costs of schools were financed through student fees, and, as a result, families were carrying a burden of educational costs. Closely tying community wealth to school administration disproportionately impacts the educational opportunities of children in poor areas (Hannum, 1999). Studies of educational stratification in China support the findings of school disadvantage for children from rural areas (Connelly & Zheng, 2003; Hannum, 1999, 2003; Hannum & Park, 2002).

Parental involvement for China's development

In China, parents are being called upon to work more collaboratively with the schools to support their children's education. This is a major change for both the parents and the schools. China is currently implementing educational reforms to improve quality and efficiency in education and, as part of these reforms, parents are required to work collaboratively with their children's schools as spelled out in the *Education Law of the People's Republic of China.* Chapter VI, Article 49 of this law outlines the legal role of parents in their children's education, as follows:

> Parents or guardians of minor children shall provide their under-age sons and daughters, or children under their guardianship, with the necessary conditions for their education.
> - Parents or guardians of minor children shall collaborate with the school, or other educational institutions, on the education of their sons and daughters or children under their guardianship.
> - Schools and teachers may provide the parents of students with advice.
> - Parents are expected to work with school teachers and administrators to support their children's schooling.

At the local level, a Bu Xi city directive (2004, p. 8) stated that the importance of:

> Family education,[6] community education, and school education need to be tightly aligned . . . to help and guide parents to establish correct family education ideas, to grasp the scientific principles of family education methods in order to raise the scientific education of their children.

The Education Bureau Report cited above highlights important connections between family education, school education, and community education as critical components of China's educational reform. In order to strengthen family and school relationships, Leyi City officials have established parent education schools[7] to teach parents how to raise their children using scientific principles. My study focuses on a county that had just begun to establish parent education schools and had a strong interest in improving its parent–teacher relations.

Conclusion

According to Bourdieu's theories and China's policy-level literature, rural parents should not have the disposition nor the competency to be involved in their children's education. Currently, there is little research about parental involvement in rural China. China's current policy interest in promoting increased parent–teacher relations has opened up a space to consider rural parental involvement in their children's schooling. Given that the government wants to improve parent–teacher relationships to support children's schooling, I worked to understand how rural parents were supporting their children's schooling.

To understand rural parental involvement in China, it is essential to investigate the perspective of rural parents. Using Bourdieu's concepts of habitus, field, and capital, I focused on how poor rural parents described their role in their children's schooling. Examining how the habitus of rural parents shape their involvement and are shaped by interacting in ways to support their children's education. The context of China's current development offers a cultural, historical, and economic

Parental involvement and social class 25

perspective of how rural parents support their children's schooling. In my study, I paid close attention to both visible and invisible forms of parental involvement. Central questions addressed in this book are: How do parents themselves describe and understand their support for their children's schooling? What social interactions do they engage in to support their children' schooling? What strategies do they employ and how did they understand these strategies?

This book seeks to expand current understandings of parental involvement by presenting the mechanisms used by rural parents in China. Current research on parental involvement has identified that race or social class may influence the ways parents are involved in their children's schooling. However, what has been missing is a better understanding as to why parents engage with various forms of involvement. This book focuses on rural parents in one community to not only describe their involvement in their children's schooling but also to provide a conceptual framework for how rural parents are involved in their children's schooling. At the core of the conceptual framework in Figure 1.1 is parents holding high educational aspirations (discussed further in Chapter 3), the importance of student agency in learning (discussed in Chapter 4), parents engaged in paid and unpaid labor (discussed in Chapter 5), actively seeking information (Chapter 6), and seeking better educational environments (Chapter 7). Before discussing each of the features of the conceptual framework, Chapter 2 lays the foundation of what it means to be a rural resident and living in rural areas. This is critical to understanding how rural parents approach involvement in their children's schooling.

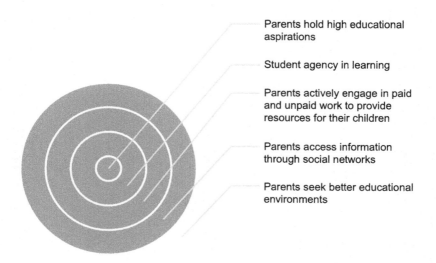

Figure 1.1 Conceptual framework for rural parental involvement

Notes

1 Other scholars have also made similar distinctions between the forms of parental involvement. A common distinction is home-based versus school-based; see Parcel & Dufur, 2001, Parcel, Dufur, & Zito, 2010; Pomerantz, Moorman, & Litwack, 2007.
2 These concepts overlap with Coleman's social capital.
3 See Suzuki (2002), Rose (2003), and Carolan-Silva (2011) for studies in other country contexts.
4 Rural parents in my study described their perception of their own parents' involvement in schooling as being limited. Their parents were busy working in the communes and expected them to take care of the household chores and did not emphasize their studies.
5 Hao, Hu, and Lo (2014) provide additional information on changing *hukou* status.
6 In pre-revolutionary times, family education meant teaching children manners, respect, and filial piety.
7 Parent schools started in China in the 1980s in response to the Compulsory Education Law of the People's Republic of China, 1985. Parent schools are seen as a piece of the larger education reform by unifying school, family, and community and by improving basic education in China. The purpose of parent schools is to link school, family, and community. Parent education schools are envisioned to improve the educational level of parents and aid parents in promoting literacy and the education of their children. Parents learn pedagogical knowledge and psychology to better understand a child's development. Parents learn that family education is a science and gain psychological, theoretical, and pedagogic knowledge to understand a child's development. For more information on parent schools, see Ma and Guo (1995).

2 What it means to be "rural"

On a cold sunny Sunday morning, I sit with Mrs. Hu on the ground in an alcove off the Hu family living room, eating sweet mandarin oranges and discussing her children's education. With the sun streaming through the windows, Mrs. Hu takes my hands in her own. She firmly cups her rough and dry hands around my own and initially rocks my hands to the left and to the right, but suddenly grips them tightly and slowly raises her head, drawing her eyes away from the mandarin orange she is peeling and looks me straight in the eyes and draws a deep breath and exhales, "As rural peasants, we have little education and can't write anything [to the teacher] . . . the *suzhi (素质)* in rural areas is not really high." She goes on to tell me that rural areas like our Zhengxing cannot keep up with urban areas. Rural residents are looked down upon and seen as backward. In my many visits to the Hu household, Mrs. Hu often began with phrases such as, "As rural peasants, we are not the same as" or "Rural peasants like me, we don't really know" or "We are not like those living in the urban areas" as part of her response to my questions about her educational background and support for her children's schooling. Mrs. Hu clearly identified as a rural peasant, and her social position as a rural resident shapes her interactions. Mrs. Hu was not alone in describing her responses from the perspective of being a rural peasant; every parent in the study spoke about how rural areas are clearly lacking quality in the rural areas in terms of physical resources, attention from the government, and also in terms of being a distinct class of people. Rural residents were very clear about their social position. This chapter is dedicated to giving voice to how rural parents speak about what it means to be "rural." Their voices echo much of the discourse of modernization, focus on the individual, and the importance of *suzhi*, and through hearing the voices of rural parents we better understand their habitus as they engage in the different fields of the home, school, and in the community to support their children's education. Specifically, we can understand both the ways parents interact, or do not interact, with schools, but also their own perspectives and how the structures of society shape parental habitus.

Parental social position

Habitus and social class

Rural parents see the world from their social position. Their lives, as rural residents and rural parents, shape the role they play in their children's schooling. In this book, I demonstrate that rural parents care deeply about their children's schooling, and their views on education are influenced by not only their social position but also the social, economic, and political dynamics around them. Moreover, rural parents have developed ways of being involved in their children's schooling that take into account the structural barriers that serve to place them at a disadvantage.

An individual's social position influences their understanding of the world. Bourdieu (1984, pp. 130–131) explains that our dispositions shape the way we see the world and that "even the most disadvantaged, tend to perceive the world as natural and to find it much more acceptable than one might imagine." The feeling and sense of one's place implies an acceptance of one's social position and limits (Bourdieu, 1985). In his description of social spaces, Bourdieu (1984, p. 130) says:

> The dispositions of agents, their habitus, that is, the mental structures through which they apprehend the social world, are essentially the product of an internationalization of the structures of the social world.

Furthermore, he believes that an individual's self-classification is the most accurate form of classification (Bourdieu, 1990). Therefore, I focus on how rural parents describe their own social position. By understanding the habitus of rural parents, we can see how they view the social world and what they view as self-evident.

Rural parent social position

Bourdieu (1985, p.724) argues that one's social class is based on the distribution of powers, which he defines as

> economic capital (in its different kinds), cultural capital, and social capital, as well as symbolic capital, commonly called prestige, reputation, and renown, etc., which is the form in which the different forms of capital are perceived and recognized as legitimate.

Rural residents have different forms of capital and engage them when they interact with schools and wider society. As discussed in Chapter 1, studies of parental involvement in their children's schooling have focused on cultural and social capital. Bourdieu (1984, p. 123) suggests that people who are in lower social positions derive some of their dispositions from those in higher social levels "towards which they tend and 'pre-tend'." Moreover, he posits that physical distance also adds to the distance between dominant cultural capital and the individual's cultural capital; he says (1984, p.124),

The distance of farm workers from legitimate culture would not be so vast if the specifically cultural distance implied by their low cultural capital were not compounded by their spatial dispersion. Similarly, many of the differences observed in the (cultural and other) practices of the different fractions of the dominant class are no doubt attributable to the size of the town they live in.

Bourdieu suggests that the physical distance between rural residents and urban city centers partially underscores the difference between the cultural capital of rural residents and that of urban residents. Additionally, rural residents determine some of their disposition in reference to urban residents. I focused specifically on rural residents in order to understand how being a rural parent shapes their involvement in their children's schooling. I interviewed rural parents whom Bourdieu would classify as having limited cultural capital because they had little experience with the dominant culture. However, rural parents live within the political, economic and social structures of China's modernizing society. I argue that these structural factors contribute to how rural parents shape their habitus and how they engage their resources to support their children's schooling. I want to understand the individual agency of rural parents to support their children's education. The socioeconomic structures shape the habitus parents and rural parents are faced with – the task of being involved and supporting their children's schooling, a field that is unfamiliar to many families.

The importance of a rural parent's social position and dispositions influences their involvement in their children's schooling. I find that based on their *diwei* (social position) in Chinese society, rural parents are critically aware of their shortcomings and discourse focused on the value of urban residents. The social and economic structure of China have shaped rural parents' educational and life experiences and influence rural parents' own habitus; moreover, their dispositions and experience with schools affect parental views of education for their children. Based on their social position, however, rural parents feel that they do not have the linguistic and cultural competencies, or *suzhi,* to support their children's schooling. Moreover, as rural peasants, rural parents are considered backward. This chapter grounds the book in terms of describing rural parental habitus. In this chapter I present six families, the Hu family, Lu Family, Zhu family, Yao family, Qi family, and Wu family to illustrate how prior experiences and rural life influence parental habitus, which in turn influences their perspective of the opportunities for their children. Rural parents experience transformative agency through their experiences living in rural areas.

What does it mean to by uneducated?

We don't make our living based on being educated. In my family, the children, the oldest started working and another entered the armed forces, and the rest have never been to school. Both my parents never attended school. In the past, in rural areas, not many went to school.

Mr. Zhu's description of his understanding and experience with the education system resonated with nearly all the parents in my study. Most of the parents in my study came from large families and grew up in households where going to school was not important or connected to one's livelihood. From his childhood, Mr. Zhu remembers being responsible for many household chores and being an important part of the family farm. His parents did not go to school and did not emphasize his education. It is clear that familiarity and understanding of the education system, including support for education, shape parental dispositions and how they are involved in their children's schooling.

Parents in rural areas have limited education. Table 2.1 shows a summary of family background statistics from the Gansu Survey of Children and Families (GSCF). Mother's average years of education is four years and father's is seven years of education. Table 2.2 provides basic family descriptive information of participants in this study, including parental education and occupation. Average parental years of education of parents in this study were similar to the average years of education of the GSCF sample, mother's average years of education is almost four years (3.69) and father's average years of education almost seven years (6.75).

What is important to note is that even though parents have attended school, all parents in the study reflected that what they learned in school is not equivalent to the content of the same grade today. Moreover, when they were growing up and going to school, they were not encouraged to study, and parents were not involved in their schooling. Tending to household chores and farm work was the household priority. Later we will examine how these dispositions toward education and involvement in children's education are shaped by the changing economic and social conditions toward having dispositions focused on cultivating children's educational learning.

Table 2.1 Summary of family background statistics

	Mean	Standard deviation	Minimum	Maximum
Mother's education level (n = 1,863)	4.32	3.45	0	13
Father's education level (n = 1,864)	7.12	3.64	0	29
Number of kids in the family (n = 1,865)	2.33	0.72	1	6
Family wealth (n = 1,865)	10,649.29	36,247.48	120	974,900
Mother in the home (n = 1,863)	0.98	0.16	0	1
Father in the home (n = 1,864)	0.78	0.41	0	1

Source: GSCF-2 Mother and Household questionnaires (2004; https://china.pop.upenn.edu/gansu-survey-children-and-families-gscf).

Table 2.2 Basic family background descriptives

Family	Number of children and composition	Grade in school	Mother's education	Father's education	Mother's occupation	Father's occupation	Educational aspirations
Wu (Wu Shizhuang)	2, 1 daughter and 1 son	8th grade 6th grade	Junior vocational college	High school	Preschool and Chinese junior high Teacher	Farmer	College
Ao (Ao Jinhui)	3, 2 daughters and 1 son	9th grade 6th grade 4th grade, repeated 1st grade	4th grade, 1st semester	5th grade	Farmer and store owner	Farmer and store owner	College
Wen (Wen Yijin)	2, 1 son and 1 daughter	8th grade 6th grade	5th grade	5th grade	Farmer and stonecutter (temporarily)	Farmer and stonecutter	College
Wu (Wu Zimou)	2 sons	7th grade 6th grade	No schooling experience	2nd grade	Farmers	Farmers	College
Chang (Chang Bao)	1 son	6th grade	5th grade	8th grade	Farmer and pig farmer	Farmer and pig farmer	College
Ya (Ya Jingqi)	3, 1 daughter and 2 sons	8th grade 6th grade 5th grade	12th grade	8th grade	Farmer and worker	Farmer and worker	College
Gu (Gu Baodu)	2 sons	Older brother not in school, 6th grade	No schooling experience	5th grade	Farmer	Farmer	College
Zhu (Zhu Hanqi)	2 sons	6th grade 5th grade	6th grade	9th grade	Farmer, store owner	Farmer, store owner	College

(*Continued*)

Table 2.2 (Continued)

Family	Number of children and composition	Grade in school	Mother's education	Father's education	Mother's occupation	Father's occupation	Educational aspirations
Lu (Lu Xingqi)	2 children, 1 daughter and 1 son	6th grade 3rd grade	3rd grade	9th grade	Farmer	Farmer	College
Wang (Wang Zhu)	4 children, 3 daughters, and 1 son	9th grade 6th grade 6th grade 4th grade	No schooling experience	High school graduate	Farmer	Farmer	College
Gao (Gao Ling)	2 children, 1 daughter and 1 son	6th grade 5rd grade	6th grade, elementary school graduate	9th grade, middles school graduate	Farmer	Farmer	College
Zu (Zu Hongqi)	2, 1 daughter and 1 son	6th grade 5th grade	3rd grade	5th grade	Farmer, restaurant owner	Farmer, restaurant owner	College
Yao (Yao Xusao)	2 sons	7th grade 6th grade	No schooling experience	5th grade	Farmer	Farmer	College
Hu (Hu Zhuwan)	2, 1 daughter and 1 son	8th grade 6th grade	5th grade	9th grade	Farmer	Farmer, worker at local institution	College
Qi (Qi Youkang)	2 sons	Not in school, 6th grade	No schooling experience	4th grade	Farmer	Farmer, worker	College

Lawrence-Lightfoot (2004) exploring parent–teacher interactions in the United States revealed that "generational echoes" influence both parents and teachers as they are shaped by their educational histories as well as the larger societal and cultural histories that give them their place in society. Both Annette Lareau and Diane Reay studied parental involvement of parents with limited or less positive experiences with formal schools and found that these parents feel inadequate and lack confidence in working with schools (Lareau, 2000; Reay, 2000). Mr. Zhu's disposition was shaped by growing up in a family that did not value education and did not actively support his education. And in a family and community where formal education was not a natural part of growing up. Rural parents recalled that their main responsibility growing up was to help on the farm, with less emphasis on their schooling. Although many parents attended schools, their main role growing up was to help the family farm. Parents have limited dispositions to understand how schools work and the limited role their parents played in their schooling. Thus, the involvement of their own parents in their schooling was quite limited. Educational expectations were not high and there was not an emphasis on social mobility, but a sense of place in rural areas. It is important to understand parents' own educational experiences as part of their social location and how political, social, and economic structures shapes parental habitus and continues to be re-shaped as parents engage support for their children's schooling. This chapter presents the voices of rural parents to illustrate how parental habitus has been shaped by the structures around them. These include parental experiences with the education system including the lack of quality, of being uneducated, and with China's modernization discourse. These discourses define the lived experiences of rural parents and how they, as parents, support their children's schooling.

As outlined in Chapter 1, China began implementing compulsory education after 1985, when most of the parents in my study were already entering young adulthood. Compulsory education and children attending school consistently is a recent experience in these rural areas. Most parents in the study had little to some educational experience, and it was common that parents of parents in the study had no educational experience. So, parents in the study come from not only a home life with little schooling experience but also from communities where schooling is limited. And the connection between going to school and one's livelihood is not connected. In this chapter we see how parental habitus has been shaped by their educational or lack of educational experiences, and also how their habitus is shaped by their experiences and understanding of rural life and, more importantly, how rural parents adjust their dispositions as they are involved in their children's schooling. Bourdieu's (1991) concept of "habitus also provides individuals with a sense of how to act and respond in the course of their daily lives. It 'orients' their actions and inclinations without strictly determining them. It gives them a 'feel for the game', a sense of what is appropriate in the circumstances and what is not, a 'practical sense'" (p. 13). We see that rural parents have dispositions that guide their everyday life and how these shape the ways they are involved in their children's schooling. Rural parents identify as having less culture, living in areas with fewer resources, speaking a local dialect, and lacking *suzhi*, but they are not resigned or feel that their life or their children's futures are predetermined. In fact, parents in this chapter offer us a rare look into how their upbringing and the structures around them shape their habitus and also how their habitus is being shaped by their interactions with their children and schools.

Rural areas as backward and lacking, compared to urban areas

Rural parents in the study strongly emphasized the constraints of rural areas and almost always juxtaposed the conditions of rural areas with urban areas. According to Bourdieu (1991), "as an object of knowledge for the agents who inhabit it, the economic and social world exerts a force upon them not in the form of a mechanical determinism, but in the form of a knowledge effect" (p.127). The discourse on urban preference and lacking rural areas was evident in the habitus of parents as they described their perspective of the rural environment. The ways that parents discussed what they knew could be understood as their linguistic and cultural competencies with the dominant culture.

Linguistic and cultural competencies

The two main areas through which the family transmits the dominant culture to its children are their linguistic and cultural competencies (Bourdieu, 1977a). These linguistic and cultural competencies are referred to as cultural capital, which families have and are able to transmit to their children. Bourdieu believes that educational institutions are supposed to teach children how to succeed by accessing the dominant culture. However, educational institutions do not systematically transmit what is needed to children so that they can access the dominant culture. Hence, schools become the monopoly of social classes (cultured and dominant classes) who are able to access the dominant culture (Bourdieu, 1977a). The use of a dominant unifying language serves to devalue the local dialects (Bourdieu, 1991). Research in the United States and England has operationalized this relationship between families and schools and has found that families familiar with the dominant culture of schools interact differently with schools than families who are not familiar with the dominant culture (Lareau, 2000; Reay, 1998). Linguistic use of *Putonghua*, standard Mandarin, is used in schools. In rural Gansu, regional dialects are commonly spoken and referred to as *tuhua*.

Lacking school resources

Lu Xinqi's family lived in one of the villages that hug the desert that experiences severe gusty desert storms. Residents in this area all fear that the desert will eat up their land. In order to combat the voracious appetite of the desert, a tree farm runs against the far side of the village as a barrier between the village and the desert. The tree farm breeds and grows trees that are used in all parts of the area to reduce the desert dust storms and fight the desert. Unfortunately, few trees survive in these very dry conditions. Both of Xinqi's parents are farmers as well as working off-farm at the tree farm. Mr. Lu completed middle school and Mrs. Lu completed third grade. Lu Xinqi has a younger brother in third grade, and her grandparents live in their home.

In my first meeting with Lu Xinqi's father, he described rural schools and rural life in detail to me. Mr. Lu explained that on the whole, the rural environment and schools were lacking in terms of student quality, teacher quality, and parent quality compared with urban environments. He shared with me:

> Of course, the rural school environment is lacking compared to urban schools, from all perspectives. The rural teaching quality is also far behind, **our** rural students are also apathetic, and family economic situations are not good. Kids love to play, and are not successful in their education. Some teachers are able to just manage [the classroom], and are not able to work together with parents. Parents are ordinary people (老百姓) and are busy...

Mr. Lu compares the rural context of Zhengxing with urban areas and highlights the differences between teaching quality, student behavior, and family economic conditions. When he spoke he emphasized the use of "our rural students" and raised his right hand up in the air and swirled it around as if he was indicating these students around me. His use of the words "ordinary people" conjures up the discourse of rural peasants as commoners and less valued than residents in urban areas. Mr. Lu lays out an image of rural parents being busy, rural children focused on playing, and the overall lack of resources in rural areas, all disadvantaging children in rural areas. Mr. Lu goes on to describe the overall physical structure of the school to show that Zhengxing lacks resources and has low *suzhi*:

> The *suzhi* of the school is low and does not resemble a school.... I hope they fix the main gate. The facilities at the school are poor, meaning that this place is not valued by the country.... The central government values education, but we are a poor rural area and the government has not invested any money here and invests in other areas [neighboring areas]. In my opinion, Zhengxing has not received any investment and it has been like this for many years.

The use of the word *suzhi* to describe an inanimate object stuck with me after we met. I was quite familiar with the discourse of *suzhi* to describe people and groups of people who can work to improve their quality. However, when Mr. Lu elaborated on the idea to discuss the physical conditions and later human resources, I began to understand how human qualities could be transferred to inorganic objects as symbols of deficiency and neglect that shape rural parental dispositions of living with limited resources and attention. Parents spoke about how their educational opportunities were ignored or given up in order to support the family farm.

Above we can see that Mr. Lu feels that the government places importance on education and schooling; however, Zhengxing has been neglected, and years of inattention impact the schooling environment for his children. The main gate is

36 *What it means to be "rural"*

Figure 2.1 School gate

made of simple metal that does not close properly and has to be held closed by a chain lock (see Figure 2.1). To further explain how resources in Zhengxing have been neglected, Mr. Lu shares with me how his son's cracked desk wobbles and becomes unstable each time his son has to write, which is several hours during the school day. Mr. Lu says, "this definitely impacts his learning environment, this is not good" (see Figure 2.2).

Lacking teaching quality

Mr. Lu wonders out loud about how his son can learn when the conditions are so poor. In addition to the physical aspects of the school, Mr. Lu shares his views of the teaching quality. He said,

> I think on the whole the teaching quality is lacking. I can see this from the way my child does his math homework. I have discovered that it is not proper. . . . I feel that students do not understand and that the teachers have not clearly explained it to the students.

Mr. Lu explains to me that when he reviews his children's homework he notices that either the answers were left blank or they include illegible scribbles and would call the children to him. On two occasions I witnessed Mr. Lu review homework and call his son over to him. Mr. Lu sat upright and leaned down to look his son in the eye and asked him to explain the homework problem and his written response. His son

What it means to be "rural" 37

Figure 2.2 Desks and students

hunched his shoulders and shifted his weight slowly from his left foot to his right and back again staring at the homework page and mumbled a few incomprehensible words. Mr. Lu asked his son to speak loudly and clearly and to look at him when he spoke. His son slowly raised his head and quickly blurted out, " I don't know what to do." Mr. Lu felt it was the teacher's responsibility to make sure that students fully understood the concepts and his son's failure reflected poor teaching quality.

Similarly, Mr. Wu poignantly describes his perspective of rural teaching:

> If the child tests well or poorly, if they test well, then the teaching is good, if they test poorly, then the teaching is not successful. The teaching quality is not acceptable and in the rural areas we are the blind leading the blind, we cannot keep up with the modern man.

Similar to most parents in the study, Mr. Wu evaluates teaching quality based on his children's test results. He believes that if teachers performed their jobs well his children's performance on tests would show the teacher's teaching quality.[1] Mr. Wu is aware of the pace of China's modernization efforts and feels that rural teachers are not prepared; he feels that they are living in a place where the "blind are leading the blind," guiding the future citizens of China. Mr. Wu told me that rural teachers are also from the area do not have the quality to participate in China's development. Mr. Wu and I continued to discuss Wu Zimou's recent examination results.

Mr. Wu: Wu Zimou failed all his subject tests,[2] and the reason that he [Wu Zimou] didn't test well is because his foundation is not solid, so he can't keep up.
Peggy: Why do you think his performance is not acceptable?
Mr. Wu: His foundation has not been properly set up, so now he can't even follow along. Our Zhengxing is a place with no future.
Peggy: Why do you feel that Zhengxing is a place with no future?
Mr. Wu: I don't have any views; nowadays, scholarships have started to offer support for kids. It is not much use. Going to talk to the principal or teachers it is not of any use. Our rural kids do not get any of the scholarships and are not of any use for rural areas. Urban kids will respond to scholarships, but our rural kids will be scared and anxious.

Mr. Wu strongly feels that his son lacks the foundational skills he needs to succeed in schools. He further describes rural students as being scared and anxious and not being open, compared with urban students. Scholarships are being implemented to incentivize learning, but Mr. Wu believes it does not work for rural kids. Mr. Wu attended school until second grade, and his wife never attended school. The Wu family lived in Le Xin, off the main pathway through the village. The family had 16 *mu*[3] of land, which is more than most families in my study had, but the family's poor economic situation could be seen in the construction of their home, which was made of mud and thatch. There was a half wall that enclosed the family courtyard and their courtyard was open from the road. The entrance to their home did not have a metal frame but was instead made of wood with a simple latch lock. Mr. Wu once commented to me that most people do not come to his home because they only visit homes made of bricks, and usually look down on families whose homes are not made of bricks.

Consistent with Mr. Lu and Mr. Wu's assertions that the quality of schools was better in urban areas, Yao Xusao's mother, Mrs. Yao, had higher expectations of urban teachers. Even though Mrs. Yao did not know a teacher's specific education level, she assumed that it was low, based on the fact that the teacher was teaching in a rural area. Mrs. Yao told me:

That teacher has a low education level. . . . Of course her education level is low, if it were higher, she would have definitely been promoted [to an urban school], but she is a hard-working teacher. However, once she finds a marriage partner we'll never see her again.

Mrs. Yao was not alone in feeling that better teachers did not stay in the rural areas. Most parents in my study commented on their impression that teachers in rural areas were not as good as teachers in urban areas. Moreover, Mrs. Yao assumed that this female teacher would leave the rural areas upon marriage, implying that the conditions in the rural areas were not desirable.

Lacking interactions with teachers

Rural parents noted that having limited parental education shapes the way rural parents assess the types of interactions and involvement they have with teachers. Similar to findings from previous research on Chinese parents, rural parents viewed teachers as the academic experts, and therefore parents deferred to a teacher's higher position in educational matters. When I asked Mrs. Yao about her expectations of teachers, she responded:

> Illiterate parents, if they had expectations [of teachers] they would be idle expectations. These [illiterate] parents can't even help their children academically; whatever the kids say goes.

Mrs. Yao's response showed her feelings about not being educated. Mrs. Yao's social position as an illiterate person and parent shaped her understanding of her relationship with teachers and also her children. Her description of how unlikely and fruitless it would be for an illiterate parent to have expectations of the teacher because children of illiterate parents dictated the academic parent–child relationship. She felt that any expectations she would have of a teacher would be useless because she would not know what to tell teachers, that she was unable to help her children academically and, moreover her children dictated the academic conversation in the home. The child's role in their education will be discussed further in Chapter 4. When I specifically asked about the role of parents and the interaction of parents and teachers Mrs. Yao told me:

> I am illiterate. I am unable to monitor or help my children with their homework . . . I've never been to school, what good would it [interaction with teachers] do? . . . I'm not useful, I can only earn money to support him. . . . If they don't learn themselves, then there is nothing that I can do.

Mrs. Yao's description shows how her disposition of being illiterate and uneducated influenced her understanding and her involvement in her children's schooling. Moreover, interacting with a teacher was not within what Mrs. Yao considered as part of her social position or what she felt comfortable doing. She felt that she could not help her children academically but could provide financial support. Many rural parents voiced similar concern over their ability to help their children academically but felt they had the ability to provide financial support. However, a lack of education does not deter parents in my study from supporting their children's schooling, but it does shape how they engage their resources to support their children's schooling. Mrs. Yao explains how rural parents can provide financially for their children but that success in schools would be up to the children themselves, placing responsibility for learning on the students themselves.

I visited each household shortly after the mid-term examination results. All parents knew the examination results for their child and sometimes even the results of other children. Mrs. Qi told shook her head slowly as she told me that Qi Youku "failed each subject, he received 30 something in each subject? I am not sure his exact score." "What can I do? I am not educated and am illiterate, I can only say for him to study well, you say what can I do, what other options are there?". . . Mrs. Qi lamented and said,

> Those of us who are not educated, we are in a difficult place, we can't meet the *banzhuren,* we are illiterate, we don't know which room number belongs to the teacher, this is such a difficult situation, we also owe money, and sometimes they yell at us.

Mrs. Qi has never attended school, and her husband completed fourth grade. Qi Youku's older brother was 18 years old and had completed fifth grade. The family lived in the farthest village from the main road. The Qi family worked a plot of about 10 *mu* of rented land. In addition, Mr. Qi worked off-farm in a coal mind and was away from home for months at a time. Qi Youku's brother was also engaged in off-farm labor, doing construction work in the capital city. Mrs. Qi reiterates that being illiterate and poor not only shape her disposition of being unsure what she can do to help her children but also poses a physical challenge in turns of actually meeting the teacher. Rural parents are embarrassed and reluctant to seek help from teachers because they have limited literacy or are illiterate, and parents are also deterred from going to schools because they owe the school money and are not financially able to pay the school. Mrs. Qi's final description of being yelled out by teachers emerged as a fear among many of the parents. Parents were concerned about being scolded by teachers. When talking about if she has visited school, Mrs. Qi explained,

> Because I am illiterate, even if I go I don't know [or recognize] any of the teachers. They want to meet in person and having to look for one [teacher], that is the difficulty, my son performs poorly and then I'd need to find the teacher.

Mrs. Qi was fearful that because Qi Youku performed poorly in school the teacher would invite her to school to meet with her. Mrs. Qi had the feeling of being a fish out of water if they were to visit the school. Mrs. Qi understood that schools and teachers want to meet with parents when children performed poorly. But, as she noted above, her illiteracy and financial ability frighten her from going to school, along with her knowledge that she does not know the teacher. Mrs. Qi elaborated on her fear about talking with the teacher with, "we don't dare ask, and don't dare do anything, I don't even know my son's teacher. During school registration, my older son brought my younger son to register." Mrs. Qi clarifies that she does not know Qi Youku's teacher and that she does not dare set foot in on the school grounds here.

Lacking openness

Mr. Lu told me that he felt that the *suzhi* of rural students was lacking. When I asked Mr. Lu if he talks to his daughter about her schooling, Mr. Lu responded by saying, "When I ask her, she does not respond, and gives me a simple response, there is no initiative on her part. This is the way it is in rural areas, comparatively backward in thinking and just backward." Mr. Lu's response first shows how his perspective reflects the rural and peasant discourse of being backward and lacking and, second, that his daughter, a rural daughter, does not respond actively. In previous discussions with Mr. Lu, he had explained to me his idea that urban children are "open" (开朗), confident, and respond with thoughtful responses when asked a question. Upon further probing, Mr. Lu gave the following illustration of what he meant by the term "open":

> Not being open means, children are supposed to be educated in Mandarin. We speak a local dialect here, so our children are unable to express themselves [at school]. Sometimes what they read in books, there is a misunderstanding, because what is in the books is not connected to their everyday lives. Therefore, [they] cannot express themselves. Writing an essay, for example, they [rural students] are just lacking compared to urban students. The facilities and resources in rural areas are not as good as urban areas.

Mr. Lu's strong emphasis on how rural areas and schools were lacking, when compared to urban areas and schools, resonated consistently with all the parents in my study. But, it was Mr. Lu's ability to distinguish the reasons why rural children were not able to be "open" that was most striking to me. Mr. Lu captured the inequality between urban and rural areas; how the national curriculum and language were geared toward children in urban areas and how this obviously disadvantaged rural children. Children in Zhengxing speak the local dialect at home, which hinders their ability to speak and express their ideas in the language used in school, *Putonghua*. Furthermore, he described how this inequality was then exacerbated by the huge differential in resources available to urban and rural areas. Mr. Lu's description demonstrates his disposition and knowledge that urban environments offer the necessary resources to succeed in school and that rural children lack these advantages. Mr. Lu is very aware of the dominant perspective and benefits of language for his children. Mr. Lu wanted his children to have an urban lifestyle so that they would be able to speak properly and be "open."

Rural parents in the study identified that there has been a shift in one generation from a livelihood that is not dependent on schooling to one that now depends on schooling. Chinese sociologist Fei Xiaotong (1939) found that security was a dominant mentality of rural peasants and security was dependent on successful harvests. As Mr. Zhu mentioned earlier in the chapter, the culture of this community was not focused on education for their children but on cultivating a good harvest. As part of China's modernization efforts and economic progress over the last 30 years there has been incredible growth, and harvests have been successful. Rural parents in the study have lived through these changes, and now the sense of survival has shifted in two ways. First, the dispositions of rural parents have shifted from focusing on farming only to understanding that economic security and survival is dependent on education. Related to the first change is the shift from not emphasizing the importance of education for their children to making it a priority. Rural parents spoke in terms of how their children's survival depends on receiving an education.

Mr. Lu shares the imperative of having an education for his children within today's modern society. He told me:

> Getting an education is to learn a little knowledge, moral thought, to be a good person in all parts of one's life, and to have good living standards. If you do not go to school, you will not have any knowledge. Moreover, one's survival depends on having an education.

To Mr. Lu, having an education is more than just hoping that his children will be successful, education is necessary for survival in today's society. He sees the imperative of going to school and, more importantly, the consequences of not attending school. Going to school will help one's survival in society and provide for a good living standard. Mr. Lu goes onto to say:

> In today's society, even if you are willing to eat bitterness, no one will want your labor. Therefore, going to school and being educated has a large impact on one's ability to stand up in society. Today, an illiterate cannot get a job in the city because you won't understand some of the words in Mandarin. If someone talks to you in Mandarin, you won't be able to understand him or her. If you want to survive, you must have an education.

Again, Mr. Lu references the linguistic difference between rural residents and those in urban areas and the importance of Mandarin as the dominant language. In Mr. Lu's description of how he believes an uneducated person will be denied employment in the city underscores the desirable social location Mr. Lu wants for his children, and not remaining in rural areas. Using the phrase, "to eat bitterness (*chiku*)" emphasizes the hardness of manual labor and that even if one does choose to do manual labor there will not be a need for it. Rural parents understand the advantages that education provides their urban counterparts and want social mobility for their children.

Suzhi **and schooling**

Hu Zhuwan's mother told me that she often tells her children that studying is all for nothing if the children do not know how to be a person. Both parents told me about the importance of one's *suzhi*:

> Mrs. Hu: Not only do I want the kids to study well, their *suzhi* has to be good (all aspects) in the academic area. Also in terms of virtues, all of these aspects need to be good, having low *suzhi* just won't do.
>
> Mr. Hu: Learning is all about a person's character, it does not matter how much education one receives, the fullness of the soul is about one's character and ideology.... Foremost, a student must have a brain, in this area if the *suzhi* can be raised, knowledge or intellect is insufficient, student must have an ideology.... Otherwise, learning is meaningless.

Mrs. Hu viewed the home environment as playing the most important role for conveying this idea. She was speaking about the important role that families play in shaping the *suzhi* of their children. What struck me is Mr. Hu's last sentence about learning being meaningless if one does not have ideology. Mrs. Hu added, "Although my communication ability is low, but I believe that my children understand my meaning, they will definitely have ideology and work towards developing this." Mrs. Hu refers to herself as having low communication skills but knows that she is able to convey the importance of education to her children. In addition, we can see that Mr. and Mrs. Hu also viewed schooling as including more than academic learning. Mr. and Mrs. Hu use the language of *suzhi* to explain the importance of raising the quality of the individual. They want their children to have a good moral character and ideology. During the conversation, Mr. and Mrs. Hu emphasized that building moral character and supporting ideology development was both the responsibility of the home and school. Many of the parents in my study echoed the expectation that schools teach and support the moral and ideological development of their children. What is interesting to note is that rural residents view schooling as a means for social mobility but also have a more holistic perspective of the importance of schooling for their children's future.

Changing dispositions toward valuing education

Mr. Lu captures the sentiment that education was once not valued and part of the dispositions of rural parents in this rural area and has now become valued and viewed as important by families. Mr. Lu said:

> Being illiterate today is not acceptable. It is not like us [parents], if you study a little school you can get by. Those who have been educated compared to those who have not are not he same. They [children] will slowly start to figure it out.

He situates his response within the idea that illiteracy or a little education in the past was enough to get by and he sees the difference between an educated person and one with little education. Valuing education is no longer only a disposition held solely by urban parents but now by rural parents as well. Mr. Lu offers the example of private tutors and extracurricular classes as an example of the value placed on education for urban kids. He tells me that in the city, families value education more. When asked how he values education, Mr. Lu responded:

> Nowadays, we all value (education), but hiring a tutor is beyond our ability and we are too remote to have tutors. Moreover, our own educational levels are low . . . we can't understand the lessons.

Mr. Lu continues to deepen our understanding of the resources that shape rural parental involvement in their children's schooling. Mr. Lu is critically aware of his limited educational experience and understand that private tutors can help his children and is willing to pay for tutors, but very few tutors are available in this remote areas. Again, reflecting the remoteness of where rural parents reside, beyond the reach of educational resources. Thus, demonstrating how structures exist that further limit the educational opportunities in rural areas, but does not signify that rural parents are not involved or uncaring of their children's education. In fact, this is evidence of the contrary that rural parents, who not only have limited education, few economic resources, and have grown up where parental involvement and support for education is not valued, now understand that they can be involved in their children's schooling by seeking out academic support for their children but find that none exist.

For parents who have limited education like Mrs. Qi, receiving formal schooling is viewed as very important for living in today's society. Mrs. Qi explains:

> In today's society, not being educated is not an option because if you want to go out and work you won't be able to. To speak of nothing else, if you are not literate you won't even be able to tell the difference between the bathrooms [men/women]. Bathrooms are all written in English, if the children do not recognize the words they will not know which bathroom to use. If you have a little bit of education you will have a way out and being out in the world also allows one to by more agile and resourceful.

Several other parents also gave examples of how locating a bathroom was challenging in urban areas. Mrs. Qi offers an example of the practical importance of literacy in not only Mandarin, but also now English. Using the example of a bathroom strikes at the heart of necessity, contrasts urban and rural (modern and not-modern), and the importance of context.[4] Mrs. Qi's explanation of how education offers one a "way out and being out in the world" speaks to the idea that one can leave the village and go out into the urban areas. Moreover, that any amount of education will help make a person more "agile and resourceful." As someone who has never been to school, Mrs. Qi understands the significance of formal schooling for her children and is actively involved in their schooling.

Conclusion

In this chapter, we first see that rural parents are not bumbling country bumpkins, and this is essential to understanding that rural parents clearly see how their habitus is structured and the challenges of what being rural means to parents. The meaning of rural frames how rural parents are involved in their children's schooling. Parents are still concerned about survival and security, and view education as important for their children's survival in the modern society. Rural parents have also been shaped by the discourse on the advantages of urban areas and the lacking backwardness of rural areas. Parents almost always situate the rural context in terms of urban areas. In describing their ability to support their children's schooling, rural parents were self-deprecating and viewed themselves as being inferior to urban residents and teachers. Rural parents in my study describe their *habitus* and view the rural area in which they live as lacking in resources, backward, and overall having low *suzhi*. Parents describe what it means to be a rural person living in rural areas including the sense that rural areas are lacking and backward. One way of viewing parent views of a sense of being lesser than urban areas is be to feel that rural parents are resolved to their lot in life. However, in the following chapters, we will see how rural parents are active, informed, and engaged in their children's schooling. These perceived shortcomings fueled and motivated parents to support their children's education and hold high educational aspirations for their children.

Other scholars have also noted similar levels of educational aspirations for urban and rural Chinese parents (Kipnis, 2011a; Kong, 2010; Murphy, 2004a). However, parents in my study do not echo prior research that education is valued and by rural parents universally. In fact, parents describe a different narrative where schooling was not valued for them, which shapes their understanding of the value of education. This is quite interesting because much of the educational stratification literature has shown that children from families with higher social class backgrounds are more likely to aspire to higher educational levels than those from lower social class backgrounds (Sewell & Shah, 1968). Fan's (2001) study of parental involvement and academic achievement found a positive relationship between family socioeconomic status and educational aspirations. Rural parents in my study understand their own educational limitations: however, their own habitus does not indicate low levels of parental efficacy in involvement as parents focus on the positive support for their children's education. Finally, in terms of how parents view the development of *suzhi* in their children, I find that rural parents want academic learning for their children but also moral and ideological development and ideological development. Rural parents did not want their children to endure hardship and wanted them to leave the rural areas, which will be discussed further in the next chapter. Schooling was viewed as a means for social mobility, but parents also described schooling as important for a child's moral and ideological development. Rural parents wanted to raise their child's *suzhi,* and as Murphy (2004a) pointed out, this individual approach removes the responsibility from the state or society to help rural residents. Rural parents understand that the responsibility for raising the *suzhi* of their children lies with them.

Finally, rural parents described the importance of education in today's society and often discussed the lack of emphasis on education in their own childhoods. Moreover, they gave stark illustrations of the changes in China's economic development from their childhood to the present day. The combination of these social and economic changes in rural China have had a profound impact on how rural parents are portrayed as well the habitus of what it means to be rural parents. This chapter offers a glimpse into how rural parents see their social position in society, which serves as the foundation of how parents support their children's schooling for social mobility. In the next chapter, why and what parents aspire for their children will be discussed. In this particular rural area, contrary to prior research, the importance and value of education is emerging and is only recently being endorsed as necessary for children's futures.

Notes

1 Teacher evaluations are typically based on student performance on examinations or entrance into the next level of schooling. Parents thus believe that the failure of students is related to teacher quality.
2 School records from his teacher confirmed these test results.
3 A *mu* is a measurement and is equal to 1/15th of a hectare. There are about 3885 *mu* in a square mile.
4 In a village, bathrooms are located in two places, either in the small animal huts in a family courtyard or a communal small mud structure located on the outskirts of the village with a slight covering of two pits in the ground separated into two sections. The communal bathrooms typically do not have signs indicating a bathroom. One has to have knowledge of the village in order to find the bathroom. Mrs. Qi has this knowledge and lives in an environment where the use of characters, either Chinese or English, to denote a bathroom is not necessary. In contrast, she is finding that her limited education poses a challenge to finding a bathroom. Hu Zhuwan's grandmother took this idea one step further and stated "in today's society you will need a *wenping* to work in a bathroom."

3 Parental hopes and desires

Each time that I boarded the second of two public long-distance buses from the small township that I took to my research site I noticed how few seats were left unoccupied. The bus filled quickly with individuals and families carrying and transporting supplies and food from the city back to their villages. Overflowing sacks of clothes, cases of alcohol, and other household goods were stowed in the overhead baskets, seats, and on people's laps. As the bus meandered along the road, passing small squat buildings and giving way to open land, fellow bus riders asked me where I was going. When I told them that I was going to Zhengxing Primary School, my fellow bus riders would ask if I was a teacher. I would explain that I was not a teacher but a researcher interested in understanding rural family life and children's schooling. They could not understand my interest in rural life. My fellow bus riders were not the only ones bewildered by my interest in interviewing and studying the life of rural residents; most of my participants, teachers, and county officials often raised the similar questions. I usually responded by saying that we know a lot about urban residents but do not know that much about the lives of rural residents. My answers, however, never seemed to be quite satisfactory for them as they shook their heads in response. Others would tell me that urban families would not only have more to say than rural families, but were more worthy of study. Rural parents found it odd that I choose to live in a rural area when they felt that most rural residents simply wanted to leave rural life for an urban lifestyle.

As described in Chapter 2, rural parents describe rural conditions as being less developed and backward. The rural parents with whom I worked did not want their children "eating bitterness" (吃苦), and they viewed having an education and living in the cities as not only signs of success but necessary for survival.[1] Rural parents have high educational aspirations for their children and often invoked the adage of "hoping one's child becomes a dragon or phoenix[2]" (望子成龙/望女成凤) when they spoke of their reasons for supporting their children's education. Rural parents described their experiences of being a poor rural resident during China's rapid socioeconomic development and how they believed that education was a necessity for living in today's modern society.

In this chapter, rural parents strongly held high educational aspirations for their children because they wanted their children to "walk out" of the village, broadening their children's perspectives, parents did not want their children eating bitterness, and leaving the village was a sign of success and social mobility. Holding high educational aspirations was central to rural parent's involvement in their children's schooling. As discussed in the previous chapter, rural parents in my study have experienced many social and economic changes during their lifetime and perspectives towards formal schooling including parental perception for the value of education for children and their future. The development and modernizing discourse clearly favors urban life and work influences parental beliefs that children need to walk out of rural areas.

"To walk out"

During one of my first chats with Mr. Zhan, the district education leader, he told me that rural parents have one thought, and that is to have their children "walk out" of the rural areas. Mr. Zhan explained to me that after the agricultural production brigades were dissolved, many rural parents participated in basic agricultural trainings.[3] He believed that these trainings stimulated parental interest in learning and encouraged parents to have high educational expectations for their children to exit the rural areas.[4] Mr. Zhan's words resonated with findings from other studies in rural China, where parents' desire social mobility for their children (Kipnis, 2001; 2011b). Past studies have found that rural parents hope their children will leave the countryside (Thogerson, 2002; Murphy 2004a); that rural parents hope education will help improve their children's future; and that education will be able to help their children secure employment outside of the village (Chi & Rao, 2003). Farming was associated with hardship and having low *suzhi,* and parents wanted to a better life for their children Murphy (2004a). "To walk out" out of the village means being educated and leaving the rural areas and working non-farm jobs (Chan, Madsen, & Unger, 1992; Murphy, 2004a).

In contrast to Mr. Zhan, other educational leaders, including the school principal and education bureau leader, warned me that I should be careful of the "hoodlums" that just sit around all day. These "hoodlums" were young people, mostly young men between the ages of 15 and 19. As I walked between villages and down the main township road, I noticed these young men squatting and chatting amongst themselves. They were not harming anyone or anything. However, they were clearly viewed as troublesome because they were not doing anything. Most of them had completed compulsory education and did not want to work on the farms and had not yet left to work (*dakong*) as migrant workers. Rural parents in my study were afraid that their children would become a hoodlum and not walk out of the village.

Within the parental involvement literature, the importance of parents holding high educational aspirations has emerged as having a positive influence on both children's learning outcomes and occupations (Entwisle, Alexander, & Olson,

2005; Dauber, Alexander, & Entwisle, 1996). MacLeod's (1987) work with low-income youth suggests the mediating effect of occupational aspirations between socioeconomic structures and individuals in social reproduction. MacLeod (1987) suggests that educational aspirations "bridges over the theoretical rift of structure-agency dualism" (p. 20). Holding high educational aspirations is an important component of parental involvement, and precisely serves as invisible parental involvement in their children's schooling. In Chapter 2, parents did not experience an atmosphere where their academic learning was valued in their homes. Parents in my study did not feel that their own parents held high educational aspirations for them or wanted them to walk out of the village. However, through their lived experiences having limited education and eating bitterness (吃苦) of working in the fields and living in rural areas, parents in the study share why they value education for their own children. This chapter shows the not only the parental habitus of holding high aspirations for their children and the hope for social mobility, but also what walking out of the village means to rural parents.

Educational aspirations

Rural parents in this area now hold high educational aspirations for their children. Figure 3.1 shows mother's educational aspirations by gender in the Gansu Survey of Children and Families (GSCF) in 2000 and 2004. We can see that in both years, most families hold high educational aspirations for senior high school and beyond for both their girl (67% in 2000; 80% in 2004) and boy children (78% in 2000; 85% in 2004).

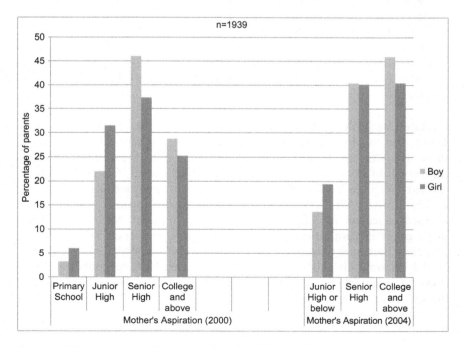

Figure 3.1 Mother's educational aspirations in 2000 and 2004 by child's sex

Parents in my study held even higher educational aspirations than the survey data results, every parent wanted their children to attend college. Mr. Lu told me his educational aspirations for his daughter, Lu Xinqi are

> very high, but it depends on if she can do it. In this day and age, the more education the better, at the very least she must graduate from a university. Then, finding a job or anything she wants to do will be much easier.

Mr. Gao's told me his educational aspirations for Gao Ling: "My aspirations are great, just have to see if they can become a reality, I want her to get into college for sure." Every parent in my study held college aspirations, regardless of family background or student academic performance.

I asked Mr. Gao how he conveyed the purpose of education to his children, he shared his social and cultural understanding of the role of education. He believed that educating oneself would help the family and his country, and that his country needed educated people. He described to me how he conveyed to his children why they needed to study:

> I tell them not to treat studying as if they are completing a chore. Studying will be beneficial to themselves, their family, and the country. In the future, the country surely needs human capital. I tell them, "you need to study well so that your work will be important. We [parents] are not educated, every day we engage in manual labor, after one is educated, one won't have to endure bitterness." I tell them, "after they have tested into college, then, they will be able to use their mind to work, and mind work takes a lot of energy. But, the amount of energy needed [to work] is less than what is needed for manual labor. At least, they don't have to labor under the sun.

Mr. Gao communicated to his daughter the importance of education for herself, family, and country. He was able to talk about the differences he saw between those who were uneducated and conducted manual labor and those who used their minds to work. The idea that education helps oneself, family, and country is often referenced in policy documents. Mr. Gao's attitude recalled the language in *The Decision on the Reform of the Education Structure of 1985*, which stressed education for improvement and modernization. Mr. Gao used this language of modernization to describe his desire to support their children's education no matter what. It appears that Mr. Gao had internalized the reasons he did not want his children working on the farm. Echoing policy proclamations, Mr. Gao defined getting a job that required using one's mind as being modern and a part of the modern economy. He wanted his children to earn their living using their minds, not their brawn, and education was the key to achieving this goal.

Parental hopes and desires 51

Gao Ling's family lived in the Lu village about two kilometers from school. Mr. and Mrs. Gao had both received formal schooling, Mr. Gao graduated from middle school and his wife completed primary school. The family of four had nine *mu* of land. Mr. and Mrs. Gao both worked temporary jobs as day laborers. Gao Ling was a high-performing child who had a younger brother in third grade. The Gao family lived in a small family compound made of mud and thatch. The courtyard did not have room for planting fruits or vegetables. The home consisted of one main room that served as the bedroom, kitchen, and living room with a bed, sofa, table and chair, coal stove, and a television.

Education for social mobility

In discussing Mrs. Zu's own educational experiences, she told me how school was different nowadays than when she attended school. Mrs. Zu did not complete primary school because she was needed in the home and Mr. Zu completed middle school. Mrs. Zu told me:

> School was different for me than it is today because today, students [families] have more money and are much better off. Before, we didn't have anything to eat, kids these days eat things that I have never seen before. In the past, the living standards were not good. I often tell my children that the snacks that they eat are snacks that I've never even seen before . . . I completed fifth grade and did not go on . . . Nowadays, kids [her children] who are as old as they are don't do any chores, [when I was their age] when we returned from school we had to cut the grass and tend to the fire. Today, my children come home and eat their meal and when they finish eating, they go out and play. When we were 7 or 8 years old we helped our mother prepare meals, wash clothes, and fetch water. Children today do not do any of it.

The social and economic conditions had changed since Mrs. Zu was a young child. She contrasted the living standards of her childhood with those of her children. This background information about how Mrs. Zu viewed both the economic and educational changes in her life reflected her observation of China's changing economy and the necessity for an education. Her comparison between how she did not have enough to eat as a child, living barely above subsistence levels, and how her children have snacks to eat (going beyond meeting a minimal level of food intake) clearly showed one aspect of her experiencing China's economic changes. She had lived through the experience of not having enough to eat to now being able to sufficiently provide nourishment for her children. In her description of her children's eating habits and leisure activities, we can see that she ensured that her children were comfortable. We can also see the importance that Mrs. Zu placed on her children's education, in comparison to her own time as a student, by the absence of children's chores in the Zu family.

The Zu family lived along the main road in their small auto/truck part shop. During my visits with the Zu family, there were very few clients visiting the store. Mrs. Zu told me that the family's economic situation was better now than when she was younger, but that sales have been declining ever since the railroad was completed. The railroad diverted much of the truck traffic, diminishing the demand for truck parts. So, Mrs. and Mr. Zu would often work off-farm temporary jobs to help provide for the family. In addition to owning the store, the Zu family owned 6 *mu* of land.

Later in our visit, Mrs. Zu and I talked about her schooling experiences. She connected her experience in schools with her expectation of education in today's modern world. She explained:

> In the past, the teacher had many students, so they were only concerned with teaching their lessons, not like today where teachers "have a firm grasp of" (抓) students. In the past, if students performed poorly, then they performed poorly, parents didn't care, if they studied they studied. This is unlike today's parents, we all want our children to study and succeed. In this day and age, if a child does not have an education they won't be able to live. In our day, there were many uneducated children, more than those who went onto middle school, and there were none that went onto high school.

Again, Mrs. Zu emphasized the important role that education plays in one's life. When she was a child, parents and teachers did not place a strong emphasis on education. The government's recent reforms supporting compulsory education can be seen by the high value placed on education by parents and teachers in this area now. Mrs. Zu saw education as a requirement for her children to "live" (活) in today's society and this motivated her to support her children's education. Mrs. Zu's description of wanting her children to achieve educational success, since to her, education now had economic implications. She believed education had become a cultural norm. In a subsequent discussion with Mrs. Zu, she described how it had become the norm in this area to have students enter high school and that even a few have gained entry into higher education.

Yao Xusao lived in Le Xin village, about four kilometers from school. Yao Xusao was a low-performing student and had previously repeated third grade. He had one older brother in seventh grade, who had also repeated a grade. Mrs. Yao had never been to school and Mr. Yao only completed fifth grade. Yao Xusao's family only had 6 *mu* of land for a family of four. They had so little land because the government divided the land and parceled it out after the Mr. Yao's older brother was born.[5] When you enter most rural homes, there is an open courtyard for a small garden and bedrooms and kitchens are usually located off the main courtyard (see Figure 3.2). The poverty of the Yao family was reflected in their home; it did not have a courtyard and consisted of only two rooms – one for a kitchen and the second for a bedroom/living room. In addition to farming their land, both Mr. and Mrs. Yao worked odd jobs off-farm in the local area to support the household. Money was a constant topic around their house. In fact, Mrs. Yao personally went to register the children at school this year because she was concerned that the children would lose the tuition money while walking to school.

Parental hopes and desires 53

Figure 3.2 Courtyard

If the children lost the money, they would not be able to attend school that year. Mrs. Yao expressed how scared she was of going to the school to register her children because she was not educated, but Mrs. Yao felt having an education was a matter of survival for her children and put her own fear aside to confront school personnel. Mrs. Yao often talked with her boys about their educational aspirations, homework, test grades, and the opportunities being educated would afford them to walk out of the rural areas.

Mrs. Yao had an intimate understanding of the importance that education played in a person's life. She described to me how the simple fact that she could not sign her own name placed her at a disadvantage and how this related to how highly she valued education for her children. She told me:

> [I want] them to be educated because it benefits one's self. It is to say that wherever you go out to work you'll be able to see the benefit of it. If you have a graduation certificate you can take that with you and use it to obtain a job . . . I've never been educated, I don't know how to write anything, it makes life so difficult. If they [her children] are educated then they can write whatever they want and won't have to beg anyone. They will simply be able to write what they need. When I think about it, I feel terrible, my parents were not able to support my education and I can't even sign

my own name. I am 39 this year, and have never been educated, I can't even engage in simple business transactions.

Mrs. Yao's description of how strongly she felt about education illustrates her experience of China's modernization. Her experiences as an illiterate woman has influenced her understanding of the purpose of education and motivates her to support her children's education. First, she felt that an education would empower her children so that they would be able to write anything they wanted and not be beholden to others. Second, Mrs. Yao saw education and more specifically, the physical paper of a graduation certificate, as a tool that her children could wield to gain employment in the modern economy. They would have options for work and social mobility. She was saddened that her inability to sign her own name and felt that it hindered her ability to interact in modern small business opportunities.

"Hoping one's child becomes a dragon or phoenix"

During my first visit to Ya Jingqi's house (see Figure 3.3), I found Ya Jingqi's mother outside, putting leavened bread in a communal oven near her house. She looked at me suspiciously when I asked if this was the home of Ya Jingqi, but her pursed lips gave way to a smile when I told her who I was and why I was at her house. She invited me into the main living area of their home. As I entered the courtyard there was one room to my

Figure 3.3 House

right and the main row of three rooms straight ahead. The room on the right was the kitchen. The row of three rooms included a storage room for food, a bedroom, and the main bedroom and living room. In the living area, there was a television tucked in the corner, a bed in the opposite corner, and a coal stove in the middle of the room. Mrs. Ya pulled out a couple of stools for us to sit upon as we huddled around the coal stove. These basic household items reflected an average economic situation for the Ya family. During one of our meals together, Mrs. Ya shared with me a large three-foot urn full of pickled carrots and cabbage. Mrs. Ya explained to me that the family would eat these vegetables all winter alongside a little rice for lunch and dinner. It was just the beginning of December and Mrs. Ya told me she was already tired of eating the same thing each day. The Ya home was located near Zhengxing primary school and near the heart of the main street. Ya Jingqi's parents were a little unusual because his mother had a higher level of education than his father. Mrs. Ya graduated from high school and Mr. Ya graduated from middle school. Ya Jingqi had two siblings, including one older sister and one younger brother. The family had four *mu* of land for a family of five. In addition to farming the land, Mr. and Mrs. Ya both worked off-farm as day laborers. Mrs. Ya explained the importance of working construction jobs and any paid labor jobs because the family had just converted their mud and thatch home into one with tiles and bricks.

In our discussion about her educational aspirations for her children, Mrs. Ya told me that rural parents try the best that they can do. She told me:

> It is like this – we do what we can, we are all the same, we hope that our children will become dragons. . . . We all feel this way, we all want the best for our children's education, so that they will learn better, so that they will stand up. My hope is that all three of my children will go to college.

Having been educated herself, Mrs. Ya wanted her children to be successful in school and to improve their social position. Rural parents were well aware of the important role that education played in securing employment and a better place in today's society. It was interesting that Mrs. Ya used a common adage to express her desire for success for her children and then defined that success as the modern-day goal of receiving a college education.

One Friday afternoon, I walked home with Wen Yijin and her friends. We walked the four to five kilometers up the winding road to Le Xin and chatted about their favorite subjects and they told me jokes. When we arrived at Wen Yijin's house, we entered the courtyard walk through a metal doorframe and I noticed the small courtyard to the left. The house compound had three rooms, a kitchen, and two bedrooms that also doubled as living areas. We entered the first bedroom/living room to the right through a curtain of heavy blankets. Mr. Wen had just finished eating and was slowly hobbling back to the *kang* (see Figure 3.4)[6] to rest when we walked into the room. He had recently injured his foot while working at the stone cuttery and was not working. Mrs. Wen was

56 *Parental hopes and desires*

Figure 3.4 Kang

currently working at the cuttery in his place. Mr. and Mrs. Wen worked off-farm in addition to working the family's 12 *mu* of land.

This particular Friday was the day when mid-term examinations were returned to students at the middle school. About half an hour into our interview, Wen Yijin's older brother returned home with a friend, and Mr. Wen asked him how he did on his mid-terms and asked to see the results. Mr. Wen saw that his son did not pass a few subjects and asked him why he did not pass. What was wrong? Why did he do so poorly? His son did not say much, fixed himself a bowl of *sa fan*,[7] and ate lunch. Mr. Wen repeatedly questioned his son about his low grades. Mr. Wen told his son that he wanted him to "become a dragon" and that he must study hard to achieve this goal. Mr. Wen's mother cleaned up the lunch dishes and whispered in her grandson's ear a few words about the importance of becoming a dragon to his future. Rural parents were well aware of the important role that education played in securing employment and a better place in society. In his discussion with his son, Mr. Wen reiterated the importance of education for his future and how he needed to study in order to become a dragon. Rural parents have a strong desire for their children to succeed and are aware that the effort needed to achieve these aspirations lies with their children.

Mr. Wen told me that his educational aspirations for his children are: "The best is to go to college, to not return home to farm the land." Mr. Wen's aspirations resonate with the findings of previous scholars in rural China, that parents want their children to go to college and to be employed in off-farm labor. Mrs. Wen had completed fifth grade and Mr. Wen had completed sixth grade and desired more for their children. They told their children

> to be studious, so when they are educated . . . they will have a better life. When they "出人头" *chu ren tou* (succeed) they will go out into the world with their education.

Mr. and Mrs. Wen describe how holding high educational aspirations and the desire for their children "to walk out" signify success in the world. Moreover, being successful would also "reduce the burden on society; if they dropout it is society's burden, right? If you can get them to study more and move up, they will raise up their educational level and will be successful," said Mr. Wen. Mr. Wen makes a subtle reference to success as social mobility and the importance of the raising one's individual *suzhi* through education.

"Eating bitterness"

Rural parents showed a strong interest in shielding their children from experiencing hardship in their lives. Parents held high educational aspirations because they understood the kind of work available to those without an education. Mrs. Yao's own experiences as someone who had no education and who had eaten bitterness drove her to protect her son from having to face a difficult life. When Mrs. Yao and I chatted about suitable jobs for her son, she expressed her opinion that without education, one's lot will be to eat bitterness. Mrs. Yao shared with me her views about her son's future, "[I] can't tell what he'll do, but he will eat bitterness in his job . . . if he doesn't get an education, he'll eat bitterness." Mrs. Yao explained to me that she did not want her son to eat bitterness. Mrs. Yao often wept during our meetings about her concerns and fears about her son's educational and occupational future. After the sixth-grade final district examination, Yao Xusao ranked 228 out of 230 students.

Mrs. Wu, Wu Jingqi's mother, eloquently explains that she holds high educational aspirations because if her children are not educated, "they will eat bitterness and negotiate daily with the land." The imagery of negotiating with the land and eating bitterness conjures up the image of the daily difficulties of coercing the dry and hardened land in the village (see Figure 3.5). On my trips to the field with parents, I watched as parents used their bare dry hands to turn the soil. Mr. Wu follows up by saying, "Exactly, to eat bitterness. Today, peasants need to be educated, scientifically to tend to the land." Mr. and Mrs. Wu emphasized that education was important for farm work to learn the scientific and proper way to improve the land. Mrs. Wu emphasized that, "It does not work if you are not educated and trying to work the land." Mr. Wu added, "That is why the nation developed nine years of compulsory education, they want to raise the level of people's *suzhi*." Mr. and Mrs. Wu want their children to "walk out" so that they

58 *Parental hopes and desires*

Figure 3.5 Farm plot

do not have to "eat bitterness." Mr. and Mrs. Wu do not want their children to suffer, and this strongly shapes their educational aspirations for their children.

Broaden horizons

Parents held high educational aspirations for their children to "walk out" so that they could broaden their horizons. Rural parents wanted their children to open their eyes. Mr. Wu hoped that leaving the village would open Wu Zimou's eyes, although he had his doubts about Wu Zimou's ability to walk out. Extending this sentiment, Mr. Chang told me:

> I don't want Chang Bao to *dakong* (work) I want him to have a stable *chengshi gongzuo* (city job). If he can't really get into really study. I don't want him to stay in this area and live like us. I want him to go out and have more opportunities. You can't do anything here, all day long we *dunzhe* (蹲著) here. Not much to do. Chang Bao hopefully he can go out, have a job, and not have a job, go out. Young folks don't understand and stay here. I want him to go out . . . If you don't go out to look around then you will be blind. Right now we only know to farm and hope that the next generation takes it forward. We hope that he does better.

Mr. Chang makes a clear distinction between work and a job and does not want Chang Bao working. To work (*dakong*) is unstable work that is typically acquired on a daily basis with low and unreliable payment, and a city job (*chengshi gongzuo*) is a stable urban job that provides a steady stream of income. Even if Chang Bao does not have a job, Mr. Chang still insists that Chang Bao goes out to see the world so he will not be blind anymore. In addition, Mr. Chang does not want Chang Bao to stay in the local area if he will just be idle (*dunzhe* 蹲著), recalling the hoodlums that hang around the local area perched atop the banks of the road, idly waiting and wasting time. Mr. Chang does not want Chang Bao to waste his future. Underscoring the aspirations of rural parents, Mr. Chang wants his son to "walk out" so that he can have a better life than Mr. and Mrs. Chang.

Educational achievement and mother's educational aspirations

All parents in the study held high educational aspirations for their children to attend college, and this served as the core of their involvement in their children's schooling. Regardless of children's academic levels or parental educational level, parents in the study held high educational aspiration. Figure 3.6 shows mother's educational aspirations for children aged 9 to 12 in 2000 by gender and educational achievement in math and Chinese. It is clear that for boys, higher academic achievement in math or Chinese is correlated to higher mother's educational aspirations. For example, a math or Chinese score of 60 is correlated to educational aspiration for primary school, while a math or Chinese score of 70 or higher is correlated to high school or college educational aspirations. For girls, the results are similar in terms of higher scores correlating with higher mother's educational aspirations. However, mother's educational aspirations are lower for girls than for boys who score 70 points on math or Chinese. For girls, 70 points on math or Chinese is correlated with mother's educational aspirations of primary school or junior high school.

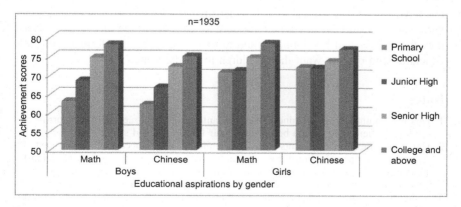

Figure 3.6 Mother's educational aspirations and child achievement (2000)

60 Parental hopes and desires

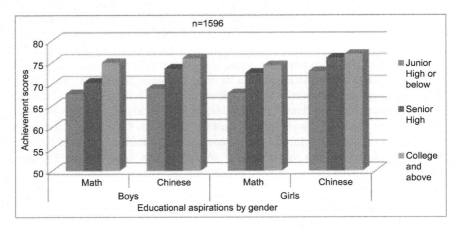

Figure 3.7 Mother's educational aspirations and child achievement (2004)

Figure 3.7 illustrates the same relationship of higher educational student achievement and mother's educational aspirations in 2004 for children aged 13 to 17. Across both girls and boys, a student math or Chinese score of 73 or higher is correlated to mother's aspirations of senior high school or higher. However, for girls in Chinese, a score of 72 is correlated with mother's educational aspiration of junior high school of below.

Conclusion

This chapter clearly shows that parents in this area now hold high educational aspirations for their children within the context of China's rapid socioeconomic development. Rural parents understood the importance of attaining a high-level of education so that their children would be able to "walk out" of the village, not have to "eat bitterness," and broaden their perspectives. The rural parents with whom I worked wanted their children to walk out of the rural areas because they themselves had lived a harsh and difficult life of being a farmer with little education and did not want their children to do the same.

Notes

1 This is a commonly used Chinese idiom meaning to live a grueling life of sorrow and servitude. There is a sense a bondage to their farm work and social class.
2 This adage means that parents want their children to be successful. In the past, the dragon was a representation for the emperor and the phoenix was a representation for the empress. Thus, parents aspire for their children to attain a higher social class, with the emperor and empress representing the highest possible class.
3 In the 1980s, agricultural production in this area was divided up into production brigades, which were the equivalent of natural villages, but were later disbanded as part of the rural economic reforms.

Parental hopes and desires 61

4 Lin (1993) also suggests that as a result of the change to the rural responsibility system, rural parents became more aware of the importance of knowledge and skills.
5 Under China's Property Law the state or village collectives own land. Individual farmers do not own farmland, but have the rights to use and manage the land. Farmers currently have a 30-year land contract. It is officially known as the first-round contract. After the first round is completed, farmers will be able to extend their contracts for another 30 years.
6 A wooden sleeping platform commonly found in rural homes.
7 A mixture boiled of rice and flour. This mixture of predominantly flour is a staple for most rural residents in this area because it is the most economical. Most families grow their own wheat and therefore have a supply of flour. Rice is not grown in the area and is an expense many families cannot afford.

4 Student's role in their own success

I arrived at around 3 o'clock[1] in the afternoon at the home of Yao Xusao for my second visit. As I entered the kitchen of Yao Xusao's modest home, I found Yao Xusao's mother sitting on a small stool beside the coal stove, slowly peeling apart paper as kindling to start the stove. I asked her if I could join her, and she invited me in to sit by the stove. As we began talking, she told me that her husband did not want her to talk to me, and that she was not supposed to talk to me anymore because she did not know what she was talking about and was wasting my time. I reassured her that as Yao Xusao's mother, she was the only person that could tell me what it was like to be his mother and about her views on his schooling experiences. After a few minutes of assuring Yao Xusao's mother that I valued her time and really appreciated her talking to me, she went into how her son was doing in school. She told me that he was not doing well and that she did not know what to do.

As she told me this, I noticed that the paper that she had been tearing was Yao Xusao's English textbook. I asked her if she knew what she was using as kindling. She told me that Yao Xusao had given it to her, and had told her that it was trash and he did not need it anymore. I told her that it was his textbook and suggested that he might need it. She repeated to me that Yao Xusao had told her that the book was not needed and she continued to tear the book apart, page-by-page, and toss the pages into the stove. As I was interviewing Mrs. Yao, I was struck by how rural parents are often depicted as ignorant and indifferent to their children's schooling in books and movies. In the Chinese movie about rural education, *Not One Less,* rural parents are portrayed as being oblivious and uncaring about their children's schooling. I open this chapter with a description of my meeting with Mrs. Yao because she represents many of the rural parents with whom I worked. At first, I felt that she was helpless, powerless to her husband and son and ignorant for tearing her son's book. However, she did not ask me to leave and continued to talk to me. As she talked to me, she asked me what she could do to support her son's education. Mrs. Yao's action of tearing apart the textbook illustrates the challenge that poorly educated parents have in supporting their children's school careers – they were uncertain about their capability, emphasized the central role of the child in the learning process, and the power shift between parents and children. As Mrs. Yao had never attended school, she was not familiar with the schools; this left her highly dependent on her children's accounts and interpretations of their educational needs. As discussed earlier in the book, rural parents' social position and habitus influenced their understanding of the educational system and their interactions – in the community and school – and their involvement in their children's schooling. This chapter highlights how rural parents shape the habitus of rural students by reasoning with the students and emphasizing role of the individual student. Through the perspectives of both parents and students we better understand how parents reason with their children about their part in learning and how students explain their motivations for studying. It is important to note that in the next few chapters the comparison to urban residents is virtually absent when rural parents discuss their active role in their children's schooling. Rural parents do not envision their role in their children's schooling against what urban parents do.

Education as a child's responsibility

In this chapter, rural parents stress the critical role children play in their own education as well as how children themselves view their role in education. As mentioned in Chapter 2, the social position of rural parents influenced the way rural parents view their support for their children's schooling, and in Chapter 3, parents seek social mobility for their children "to walk out." At the heart of how rural parents strategize their involvement and support for their children academically is the active role children play in their academic success, which is invisible to teachers. Children's agency is essential to social mobility.

Due to their own limited educational attainment, rural parents believed that their children were responsible for their own learning. That, in conjunction with holding high educational aspirations for their children, children played a critical role in parental strategies for their involvement in helping their children succeed in school. Parents viewed their support as secondary support, such as providing help with materials, educational expectations, visiting school events. This chapter highlights the shift of responsibility of learning to the individual and the importance of child's agency in their own learning reflecting the discourse on modernization and *suzhi*. Through the cases of six parents and four students, this chapter articulates the ways that children want to study and how parents support their studies. Parents in my study clearly felt that children have agency and responsibility for their own learning. Many parents would say, "children will study if they want to study, you cannot make them study. Parents cannot force their children to learn." However, parents could encourage their children by holding high educational aspirations and making the schooling conditions more hospitable for their children's learning. Susan Dumais (2002) explored the idea that the habitus of a child is shaped by parents. Dumais (2002) measured this by examining student aspirations for prestigious jobs, which was found to have a positive relationship with academic performance. To cultivate cultural capital for their children, parents send their children to extra-curricular activities, which are related to teacher expectations (Dumais, 2006). This chapter begins to delve into understanding how parents having high educational aspirations and placing responsibility on the children influence children's habitus for learning.

"It is up to them"

Believing that their children bore responsibility for their own learning, however, did not mean that parents did not encourage their children to succeed. Mr. Gao held high educational aspirations for Gao Ling, but noted that "when she gets to middle school, we'll see what level. At primary school, you can't tell and when it comes to schooling it will all depend on Gao Ling herself." While Mr. Gao felt that his daughter was responsible for her own academic success, he used an incentive to encourage her to do well in school. Mr. Gao told me that he tried to motivate Gao Ling at the beginning of the year by telling her that if she was able to rank in the top three of her school (all sixth graders) he would give her a prize. Student class rankings however, have recently been de-emphasized as a result of recent education reforms. However, as demonstrated by Mr. Gao's approach to supporting his daughter's education, parents still placed a great deal of value on the rankings. In Mr. Gao's description of his use of a prize to motivate Gao Ling, we can see that he placed the responsibility for learning directly on his daughter. After the fall semester examinations, Gao Ling ranked second among all sixth graders in the school and asked her father if he had been serious about a prize. He confirmed his offer. Gao Ling told her father that she wanted her prize to be a bicycle. At the end of the second semester, the final sixth grade examination, Gao Ling was ranked ninth out of all the sixth graders in the school district. Mr. Gao told Gao Ling that she had fallen in the rankings and needed to work harder because there were eight people who scored better than she did. Gao Ling told her father that she was ninth out of over 200 students in the school district. Mr. Gao made it a point to tell me that he was proud of her, but was careful to not tell Gao Ling that he was proud of her. He was concerned that showing his pride in her test results would inflate her sense of self. When I asked him if Gao Ling would be getting a new bicycle, Mr. Gao said that when the crops were ready he would use the money earned from barley sales to buy her a bicycle. He emphasized the importance of keeping his word. Mr. Gao cared about his daughter's education and used a prize to motivate her achievement. However, he expected Gao Ling to improve her ranking by herself, and he did not suggest that he was able to help her directly.

In later conversations, Mr. Gao expressed his educational aspirations and schooling for his children, underscoring the importance that his children take responsibility for their future educational success. He said:

> I have high aspirations, but we'll have to see if they can be realized, I hope that she will make it to college. . . . We'll see when she gets to middle school, you can't tell in primary school, learning is dependent on herself. . . . I feel the same about my son's learning, they both need to study well.

Mr. Gao acknowledged that even though he had high educational aspirations for his children, ultimately it would be Gao Ling's responsibility to attain academic success. His children would have to make the efforts to learn themselves in order to gain entry into college.

Mr. Wen, Wen Yijin's father, also emphasized that his children were responsible for their own education and learning. In Mr. Wen's description of the possibility of tutoring and the importance of reviewing work, he told me:

> We can't tell if it [homework] is completed correctly or not; we don't understand it. . . . This year we cannot get the year back. We cannot review his homework, if we could then we could teach her a thing or two; since we cannot, then it is up to them [son and daughter] to study and learn.

Mr. Wen knew that if he could tutor his children, it would help them academically. He is aware that his own academic limitations prohibit him from tutoring them and thus believed that his children were responsible for their own educational futures.

Although Mrs. Ya worked as a day laborer, she closely followed her children's schooling. She was unique in the study as she had completed high school and had a higher level of education than her husband. On one of my last visits to the Ya household, Mrs. Ya told me the simple way she supported her children's education: "I tell them [children] that all their learning materials, I will take care of them. Whatever books they want, I will buy. If they have any problems, I will address them, the power and responsibility is up to them." Mrs. Ya provides the learning materials and can also support Ya Jingqi with his homework, but the most important element to Ya Jingqi's educational success is Ya Jingqi himself. Mrs. Ya's explanation echoes Mrs. Yao, Mr. Gao, Mr. Wen, and all the rural parents in my study that students had the power and responsibility for their own learning.

At the end of one of my home visits, Mr. Lu looked me straight in the eye and sighed as he confided to me that children nowadays do not listen to their parents, but it was important that parents took care of their children. He said, "If you don't tend to your children now, then their academic results will most definitely be unsuccessful. The likeliness of getting into college will be very small and then getting a job [without a college degree] will be difficult." Mr. Lu's descriptions of the *suzhi*, the lacking school conditions, and perceived teaching quality all resonate with the policy and *suzhi* discourse that rural areas are lacking and backward. Despite, rural areas being backward and lacking, Mr. Lu clearly views that his role as a parent is to care for his children, and that includes supporting them through college.

In our second meeting, Mr. Lu explained to me that it is important for both of his children to succeed in school. He was aware of their recent test scores and told me Lu Xinqi's strong subject was Chinese and not math. He sighed and told me his educational aspirations for his children: "We want them to go to college, but we will have to see how they do in today's society. . . . I estimate that in 10 years roughly 80% will go to college. In today's society one needs to have an educational degree." He continued to tell me that at home they support Lu Xinqi's studies, but that "her success is up to her." He emphasized the things he could do to provide a good learning environment, such as purchasing pens and materials, but that the responsibility of her learning and future success was up to Xinqi herself. Mr. Lu worked on the tree farm behind his house with his wife and parents. He told me that in the summertime Xinqi would also help pick berries for pocket money. Mr. Lu told me that Xinqi would only pick for a couple of hours and then complain that she was tired and bored. Mr. Lu explained that having this work experience would help Xinqi understand the importance of going to school. He wanted her to know that she needed to be responsible for her future. Mr. Lu and most of the rural parents in the study would tell their children that if they did not study hard they would have to work the land. All parents did not want this for their children's future.

The idea that Gao Ling, Wen Yijin, Yao Xusao, and Lu Xinqi are on their own in learning and in negotiating the school space is similar to Annette Lareau's (2003) description of how working-class parents in her study expected their children to negotiate the academic space on their own. Lareau (2003) described how working-class families in the Colton schools defined how their children gained educational success as being:

> negotiated on the basis of the children's own ability, diligence, and overall performance in the classroom. The academic experience at school was a matter between themselves and the teacher and, to a lesser extent, between themselves and other members of the class
>
> (p. 59)

Rural parents in my study held similar views to the parents in Chi and Rao's (2003) study where rural parents felt their children's academic success was dependent upon their child's own ability and willingness to work. However, rural parents in my study explain that their own academic limitations and habitus with the educational field prevented them from engaging in the school. Moreover, rural parents in my study focused their resources to help make the academic experiences of their children more comfortable and easier for their children to negotiate. Rural parents wanted to mitigate the schooling experience so that their children would be successful.

The important role children play in their education as viewed by parents is not without challenges. As discussed above and in Chapter 2, rural parents feel limited in their ability to aid their children in schools and thus the role of parents becomes more about providing a good learning environment in schools, the home, and community (see Chapters 5, 6, and 7). However, remember Mrs. Yao saying in Chapter 2, "These [illiterate] parents can't even help their children academically; whatever the kids say goes." Mrs. Yao captures the agency of children and the shifting position of parents. As an illiterate parent who cannot help her sons academically, she feels that her sons dictate not only all the information between the home and school but must also navigate the schooling process. This is not to say that rural parents do not guide or support their children. Rural parents mobilize all the resources they can to create a positive schooling experience for their children, but children themselves must also play an active role in their own education. This chapter is dedicated to how parents view their child's active role in their education, how children themselves view schooling, and how this emphasis on children taking responsibility for their schooling demonstrates the power that comes with this responsibility.

Role of the child

Historically, children have been viewed in China as appendages of their parents and have little agency in their own lives (Naftali, 2009). Parents make decisions on behalf of their children, as children are expected to obey parents and have little say in their educational decisions. As part of China's modernization efforts, the country signed (1990) and ratified the United Nations Convention on the Rights of the Child (CRC) in 1992. Following the adoption of the Convention of the Rights of the Child, China enacted its own Law on the Protection of Minors in 1992. Naftali (2009) and Greenhalgh (2005) link the "neoliberal logic" that linked governing citizens with children. The discourse of development for creating modern citizens now shapes the way that rural parents and children view their responsibility to serve the nation.

As outlined in Chapter 1, there is a growing emphasis on the individual in China (i.e., the child, which aligns with recent changes in China's development). Murphy (2004a) has suggested that recent changes in China's economic and social policies have moved the responsibility of success or failure in schooling from the government onto families and students. Yan's (2003) work with youth echoes the emphasis on the individual for educational success or failure and not on society or nation. Similarly, Hanson and Pang (2010) found that Chinese youth believed it was their own unwillingness to work hard that led to their failure in their studies.

Educated and useful

When I first met Gao Ling, she was an outgoing girl. She approached me and asked, "When will you come to visit my house?" This was not typical of the other children in the study. All students were very happy to have me visit their homes, but no other child asked me when I would be visiting. Gao Ling had bright twinkling eyes that danced when she spoke. She told me about the importance of going to school and to do well in school for her future. In an essay, Gao Ling wrote about her view on education. She wrote, "I want to improve my future prospects and live a happy life. I want to ensure that I go to a big city and will be able to ride the bus and buy things; if I am not educated, I won't be able to do these things." It is striking how much her essay echoes the hopes and fears of rural parents in the study as well as her feelings of agency. Gao Ling aspires to walk out of the village to a big city and envisions taking a bus in the process. Her focus on the ability to buy things reflects the lack of money she has to buy things. Gao Ling finished the essay saying, "Lastly, I study because I don't want to be like those uneducated people who are often looked down upon. I want to be an honest and good girl." It is the end of the essay that underlies the importance of agency for rural students and how their dispositions are being shaped by the discourse of being educated. Like their parents, rural children see and experience the world of rural China and see the challenges to being uneducated, especially the negative treatment they receive. Gao Ling ends on a positive note that she wants to be an honest and good girl. When Gao Ling and I discussed her future, she told me that it is important for her that she focus on her studies for her future. She does not mention her parents or teachers, only herself. She is pleased when she does well in school and says that she has to buckle down and do well to leave the village. Gao Ling wants to be part of China's future development and participate in the modern economy.

When I first met Ya Jingqi he was quiet in class and a mid-performing student. However, over the year, I observed him eagerly raise his hand when the teacher called on student responses. In an essay about why he wanted to study and what he wanted to do when he grew up Ya Jingqi wrote:

> I like to study because I like to learn new things. Sometimes, I don't like to study because I have to memorize a lot of text and sometimes I cannot memorize them all. If I am in a bad mood then I can't memorize them all. Then, things change and I like to learn again.

In his essay, Ya Jingqi captures the interest students have in learning new things and the repetitiveness of textual rote memorization. At the end of his essay, Ya Jingqi wrote, "Why should I study? I have thought of this question a lot. I study because I do not want to be a useless person for my country. I want to do something useful so I want to study well. I like to learn!" Ya Jingqi's response reflects him taking responsibility for his learning for himself but also for his county. Children in rural China are being asked to take responsibility for their own education and are responding to this call from their parents and country.

Lu Xinqi was an average performing student who liked to play. She would tell me often that she preferred playing than doing her homework, which was not unusual for her age or classmates. Xinqi enjoyed going over to her friend's houses to play, and in fact, I found her at a friend's house on several visits. Xinqi did not actively complete her homework, her father had to nag at her to complete her homework. When Lu and I chatted about her school, she would explain to me that she enjoyed learning but that it was not fun. In her essay, Lu describes wanting to study "for her own knowledge and so that she can have an active thoughts." Lu explained that active to her meant that she could have her own opinions and respond well to questions. It is exciting to know that Lu Xinqi is learning for herself. She explained that she is learning new knowledge, although she may not be the top of her class. Xinqi giggled as she told me that she doesn't want to pick berries at the tree farm in the summer or ever again. She found the work boring and that she did not receive very much money from picking the berries. Xinqi does not mention that she is responsible for her own learning, but it is clear that she is learning for herself. She is comfortable with her school marks and enjoys learning new things in school.

Yao Xusao is one of the tallest boys in his class. He is quiet and I have caught him asleep in class a few times. In contrast to Gao Ling, Ya Jingqi, and Lu Xingqi, Yao Xusao is focused more on being useful for his parents than himself or his country. As he is one of the tallest students, his desk is in the back row. Xusao wrote a short essay; he wrote, "I see my parents working hard every day. The work they do is hard and they are tired. I want to learn and study so that their life can be easier." Yao Xusao captures in very few words the back-breaking work of rural farmers. Yao understands the difficulty of their work and the meager returns to their hard work. When I first chatted with Yao Xusao, he did not look me in the eye. His eyes glanced to the left and right and finally settled on the patch of ground in front of him. Yao Xusao told me that he wants to do well in school. He flicked his head back and mumbled that he wanted to help his family. Xusao was struggling in school, but he still hoped that he could improve. He wanted to get a job to support his family.

With responsibility comes power

Within the realm of education and schooling, parents place most of the responsibility of learning on their children in terms of children engaging themselves in the learning process and for negotiating the school space. However, the focus on student responsibility also leads to children dictating the information that parents receive from school, and in some cases children play a large role in schooling decisions. Placing the burden of responsibility on children for their own learning further illuminates both parental social position as well as the shifting burden of success or failure to individuals and families.

Mrs. Gao and I talked as we washed red dates. As the water swished around and around the large basin, tiny whirlpools formed. Mrs. Gao spoke with a thick accent from her local area. I had to ask her to repeat what she had said, as it was difficult for me to understand some of her words. She would smile each time I asked and say that she could understand me as I spoke proper *Putonghua*, just like on television. Then she would pause and say that I could not understand her *tuhua*. Reiterating that she had not gone to school and that this made it difficult for her to interact with others in this village. At one point, she called over to Gao Baodu to translate for her. After he translated her response to me, I followed up to query about his homework habits. She looked at Gao Baodu and asked if he had homework this weekend. Gao Baodu gave me a quick glance and then responded to his mother that he did not have homework this weekend. I had been in the school that day and knew for certain that Gao Baodu had homework in Chinese and mathematics. After Mrs. Gao and I had chatted and she went to lay out the red dates to dry, I asked Gao Baodu why he did not tell his mother the truth about his homework. Gao Baodu told me that he did not know how to do it and telling her would just have her worry about his homework. Gao Baodu was not intending to deceive his mother, but his actions demonstrate the complicated nature between parents who have relinquished responsibility for schooling to their children. The knowledge of whether homework has been assigned is the responsibility of the child, but this responsibility has huge implications if the child does not convey this information to parents, as in this case. Gao Baodu is a lower performing student and by not wanting to worry his mother, Gao is placing his own learning and future in jeopardy.

Mr. Wu explains to me that because he is illiterate and does not know all of the information, it is easy for his son to keep things from him. Wu Zimou does not share information about school with him because Wu Zimou is performing poorly and does not want Mr. Wu to know or talk to the teachers. Mr. Wu told me, "The only way I know that the teacher wants me to go to school is hearing it from other children who tell me." I asked Mr. Wu if Wu Zimou tells his father about going to see his teacher, Mrs. Gu. Mr. Wu sadly shakes his head and tells me, "No, he does not tell me." Mr. Wu is concerned that he does not know about Wu Zimou's academic situation at school and also that his son keeps the information from him. Mr. Wu suggests to me that Mrs. Gu send her messages through other kids instead of relying on Wu Zimou.

Yao Xusao's mother took willingness to support her son's education to another level. She implied that she was willing to work more, and earn more money when she told me that she wanted her son to repeat sixth grade. He had already repeated third grade, and was one of the older children in his class. She saw the benefit of repeating sixth grade so that he would be better prepared for middle school. This behavior is noteworthy because, as mentioned earlier, the Yao family was not wealthy and was, in fact, one of the poorer families with whom I worked. Mrs. Yao's willingness to have her son repeat a grade was remarkable because this choice meant that she would voluntarily pay for an additional year of schooling in spite of the economic hardship this might cause. The first time Mrs. Yao described her plan to me she was straightforward:

> I want to let him study, but I am afraid that he won't make it out of middle school. . . . I want him to repeat a year and then go onto middle school. . . . I thought this approach of him repeating sixth grade next year and then moving up after that.

Later in our discussion, she went into more detail about why she wanted her son to repeat a grade:

> Last year, they [teachers] wanted him to repeat fifth grade, but I didn't come around, so he did not repeat. I now see repeating as beneficial . . . [Last year] when I talked with the teacher, I didn't want him to repeat and he didn't want to repeat so they him moved up. Now, he can't keep up in Chinese and Mathematics.

Mrs. Yao admitted that the previous year she did not want her son to repeat, nor did her son want her to repeat. But, now she realized that repeating may be beneficial, because repeating may actually improve his overall chance of succeeding academically in the long run. This was a major shift in thinking because, in the past, she focused primarily on the price of schooling. As mentioned earlier in the book, Mrs. Yao accompanied her sons to school herself because she was afraid that if her sons lost the school tuition money, they would not be able to go to school for an entire year. Now, Mrs. Yao saw the benefits of schooling and realized the importance of paying for an extra year of schooling towards her son's long-term success.

To support her son's education, Mrs. Yao was also willing to seek tutoring, another educational expenditure that this family seemingly could ill afford. Despite the cost, Mrs. Yao discussed tutoring options:

> My idea is to have him repeat, but if he does not want to repeat, we'll see how he did [on the examination]. . . . If he definitely will not repeat, I want to put together some money to get him some tutoring. Whether he'll get tutoring I can't say. There are not teachers to tutor, the high school students who tutor middle school students are a joke, they cannot compare to a real teacher.

These comments on tutoring demonstrate that Mrs. Yao desired academic success. First, tutoring meant the willingness to pay for an additional educational expense, an expense the family could ill afford, in light of their poor economic situation. And second, their knowledge and awareness that high school tutors were not as qualified as certified teachers. These actions indicated a high-level of commitment to Yao Xusao's schooling that could not be seen by the school. However, Yao Xusao was not willing to repeat the grade. He had previously repeated third grade and was already much taller than his classmates. Yao Xusao exercised his agency in his own schooling, as he did not repeat the grade, even though Mrs. Yao was willing to pay additional fees to have him attend another year.

Role of the teacher

In conjunction with parental emphasis on the responsibility of children for their own learning, all parents made clear that parents were supporting their children and that teachers were also very important in their children's learning in schools. Recall that when I spoke with Mr. Ga about his educational aspirations and schooling for his children, he emphasized that his children are responsible for their future educational success. He said:

> I have high aspirations, but we'll have to see if they can be realized, I hope that she will make it to college. . . . We'll see when she gets to middle school, you can't tell in primary school, learning is dependent on herself.

His focus that children need to learn for themselves and that parents cannot learn for them underlines the importance of children's agency. Students must be responsible for their own schooling, but they are not alone, parents also viewed teachers as critical for their children's engagement in schooling. Mr. Gao told me:

> Parents can only "cry" or "idly watch" their children complete the homework, now we cannot coach them. We can't understand so much of their homework and we must count on the teacher to correct them. Primary teachers are powerful.

Rural parents rest much of their assessment of a child's success on the teacher. Mr. Gao explained:

> Teachers have a better understanding of each student and their personalities, ability, and also completion of homework, whether students complete their work like a task or if they do their homework seriously. Teachers need to carefully check/study, but now the classes are bigger and teachers cannot manage, but at the very least teachers should check their homework everyday. Teachers with smaller class sizes can manage better.

Mr. Gao shows his understanding of the role of teachers in his children's schooling. Mr. Gao emphasized the importance of whether students completed their "homework seriously." Many parents discussed the importance of students treating their work as a student as serious and focused. However, we can see from Mr. Gao's description that parents feel limited in their ability to evaluate when their children are being serious or simply completing a task. Rural parents in my study highlighted the importance of being serious about their studies.

Mr. Gao describes how he has observed the relationship between his daughter and her former homeroom teacher. The Gao family lives in the same village as Ms. Zhu, Gao Ling's homeroom teacher for Grades 1 through 5. As part of China's recent educational reforms, there has been a tightening of teacher qualifications. Ms. Zhu is a *minban* teacher and was encouraged to take the year off to study for the teacher qualification examination in order to changeover to a formal qualified teacher. Mr. Gao shared with me the importance of the teacher and student relationship. He told me:

> Gao Ling is doing okay in school. . . . Although Ms. Zhu is not teaching, we still have a lot of contact with her. My daughter likes her and often asks why she is not teaching. Kids like her and cares for her. This encourages her to study.

Mr. Gao went onto tell me that Gao Ling cares about her teachers and that she likes that her teachers also care for her. He thinks that changing of the *banzhuren* has been difficult for his daughter. Having Ms. Zhu as their homeroom teacher for several years has built strong feelings between his daughter and Ms. Zhu.

Having a caring teacher influences student engagement with learning, Mr. Gao said, "I can see from what Gao Ling writes in her essays that she is serious and also the corrections the teachers make that she [teacher] cares." Gao Ling tells her father that she wants to work hard and Mr. Gao views the teachers caring serve to motivate Gao Ling to be a serious student. Mr. Gao is impressed with the teachers correcting each incorrect word Gao Ling used in her essay. Rural parents would tell me that their child's performance on a test was a reflection of how well the teacher taught their child and how tightly the teacher looked after the student *"zhua"* "抓." The teacher and student relationship has a positive influence on a child's agency and engagement in the learning process. In the next chapter, parents share how they support their children's learning including the relationship between the teacher and student.

Conclusion

For rural parents, children's agency in their own learning is viewed as an important component of parental involvement and critical to their educational success. Children in the study also echoed many of the reasons rural parents want their children to be educated. Rural parents in my study have experienced many economic, social, and educational changes, and as a result they want social mobility for their children. Mr. Gao explained the importance of children taking responsibility for their learning and the meaning of being a serious student. Mrs. Ya described the material support she provides but emphasized the importance of Ya Jingqi in his own learning. Mrs. Yao provided a testament to the financial difficulties and mental model of rural parents in supporting their children's schooling. Mr. Lu described the material and life experiences that he provides for his daughter to aid her in her studies. Additionally, Mr. Gao showed the importance of the teacher-child relationship that supported his daughter taking responsibility for her own learning.

The perspectives of the students demonstrate a range of meanings for how or why they want to learn and study. Gao Ling described the challenges to being uneducated that motivate her to focus on her studies. She wanted upward social mobility to leave the village. Lu Xinqi offered insight into the joy of learning for herself. Ya Jingqi showed that learning is not always interesting but wanted to learn for himself and also for his country and society. Although he was not doing well in school, Yao Xusao wanted to continue so that he could help his parents. Xusao wanted to learn and do well so that he could relieve the burden on his parents. Xusao also demonstrated how children dictate educational decisions.

74 Student's role in their own success

As part of China's shifting governance and control to lower levels of government, the responsibility of schooling success has fallen on families and children. This chapter highlights the importance of rural children taking responsibility for their own learning as a central framework but invisible form of rural parent support for their children's schooling. Through the voices of parents and children, we can see that the success or failure of children falls on the shoulders of children; however, parents work to provide a supportive home and school environment for their children to succeed. These voices loudly resonate with the findings of Murphy (2004a) and Yan (2003) of a shifting of the burden onto individuals. Moreover, student responses offer a glimpse into how their educational dispositions are being shaped by their parents and the world around them.

Note

1 My afternoon visits usually occurred after 2:30 p.m. because children and teachers usually napped at home after lunch until 2:00 p.m. The afternoon nap is common in China; most businesses and schools are closed from 12:00 p.m. to 2:00 p.m. or 2:30 p.m. However, unlike teachers, students, and most residents of urban areas, most rural parents did not take this time of the day to nap and instead worked through this time.

5 Active rural parents' hidden work

Creating a good learning environment

In this chapter we see the active work that rural parents engage in, both inside and outside the home, to provide their children with a good learning environment. Previous studies of parental involvement commonly define or measure a good learning environment in terms of objectified capital, having a desk, having a bookshelf, and books in the home (Epstein, 1987; Hoover-Dempsey et al, 2001; Jaeger, 2011, Parcel & Dufur, 2001). In this study, parents articulate the role that learning materials play in the provision of a good learning environment for their children in the home and school. Rural parents in this study understand how the provision of schooling materials aids their children in the home and in the school. Parents actively engage in additional paid and unpaid work to ensure their children have not only the resources to study but also the time to focus on their studies. These actions are invisible to teachers as well as in the parental involvement literature.

Rural families in this study recognize their involvement in their children's schooling as working to earn financial capital, which can be converted into objectified capital (learning materials) for their children, which in turn also serves as symbolic capital to show that parents care about their children's schooling. Jaeger (2011) found that the possession of books (objectified capital) serves as a way for cultural mobility for families from lower and middle socioeconomic family environments compared with students from higher socioeconomic families. Thus, it is important to highlight that rural parents in the study are involved in their children's schooling by pursuing additional paid and unpaid work to provide learning materials to support their children's schooling. This chapter provides a deeper understanding of how rural parents view the provision of learning materials in their children's schooling. Not only do parents provide learning materials, they also relieve their children of household chores to provide additional study time. Rural parents actively work to make the home and school learning environments better for their children.

In this chapter, through the accounts of eight families, I share how rural parents conceptualize how their physical work translates into learning materials as well as learning time for their children. First, every single parent expressed willingness to work longer hours or take on multiple jobs in order to support their children's education financially and through material resources.

Rural parents understand the connection of converting their labor into what Bourdieu would call financial capital into objectified capital, learning materials for their children. Parents in this study also describe the conversion of learning materials into symbolic capital because it signals to teachers that parents care about their children's education. Parents believe that purchasing the learning materials will demonstrate to teachers that parents have the cultural capital and habitus of being serious about their children's schooling. Second, almost all the families exempted children from household chores during the school week so that the children could focus on their studies. Both of these strategies are examples of what I call invisible forms of parental involvement, families tried to create a positive environment at home that were not visible to the school. Parents hoped that the provision of good schooling materials would become evident to teachers and show their concern and involvement in their children's schooling.

Provision of learning materials in the creation of a good schooling environment

Parents actively worked to provide academic materials for their children's schooling to create a positive learning environment. As parents described in Chapter 2, their own lack of academic success limited their ability to directly support their children academically but they felt that they could purchase school supplies so their children were prepared for school. All parents in the study worked very hard to provide the necessary and expected materials for their children's schooling. Even though the families in my study struggled financially, they all said, "Whatever they need I will try to buy." Mrs. Ya described her willingness to purchase schooling materials for her three children:

> In terms of schooling, if he is lacking or missing anything, we will buy it for him. If he wants books, any type of notebook, I will buy them. Pens, notebooks used for learning, books, I try my best to satisfy these needs. I can go out and work to earn money, earn money to buy books and schooling materials [for them]; whatever they need I will try to buy. This is how it is. I hope that the schooling fees will be lower. When they [the school] purchases books, I hope they [the school] can work with the publishers to give us some discounts so it will be a little cheaper, then I would be in full support of it. Some of the teachers help out their relatives who work in bookstores by selling the books that their relatives carry in their bookstores. They end up driving up their relatives' book sales!

To provide all the learning materials needed for her children, Mrs. Ya willingly participated in off-farm work. Mr. and Mrs. Ya struggled to keep up with the learning material needs of their children, but they were determined to provide for whatever learning materials were necessary. However, Mrs. Ya questioned some of the required fees and choice of books that drove up the cost of learning materials. She knew that the education bureau had been clamping down on schools for charging miscellaneous fees. But, despite the charging of fees for review books and other study materials, Mrs. Ya was more than willing to pay these fees if they helped her children academically. Mrs. Ya never raised her concerns to the teachers or the school for fear of disrupting the learning environment for her children. It was more important to Mrs. Ya that her children had the learning materials that they needed, and she would do her best to cooperate with the school, despite the suspicious fees.

Mrs. Hu also viewed her role as supporting her children's schooling through purchasing schooling materials. Mrs. Hu felt that the provision of materials prepared them properly for class and so that the teacher would know that she supported them. Mrs. Hu's described her willingness to purchase school supplies for her daughter:

> When it comes to review books, we buy them all. If the teachers ask us to buy a particular form, we buy it. I buy everything school or academic related. If the teacher says we need to buy, we buy it.

Mrs. Hu explained that purchasing whatever teachers requested was her way of showing teachers that schooling was important to her and that she was concerned and cooperative with them. Mrs. Hu was not alone in wanting to meet all the academic needs of her children. Her enthusiasm to purchase any needed or requested material demonstrated her commitment to her children's schooling. Mrs. Hu' felt that the role of parents was to make the schooling environment more positive for their children by cooperating with teachers to provide any materials the teachers requested. In this way, teachers would treat their children more seriously. Mr. and Mrs. Hu believed that their willingness to support their children's schooling by providing material goods would help create a positive schooling environment for their children. Every parent emphasized the importance of working with the schools to make the learning environment better for their children.

Mr. Lu went a step further than Mrs. Hu and Mrs. Ya in his description of why he wanted to provide adequate pens and school supplies for his children. Mr. Lu told me that he wanted to provide a positive learning environment for his children. He shared with me the roles that he and his daughter played in her schooling:

> We hope to provide a positive learning environment. Now we take care of their books and school supplies, they have good pens, but the kids don't bring them, they bring the bad pens and are unable to neatly do their schoolwork, then the teacher criticizes them.

Mr. Lu felt that he had the responsibility to help his child negotiate the school in terms of the pens. He provided the resources for Lu Xinqi so that she would have less conflict with the teacher and would not be criticized by her teachers. Mr. Lu purchased proper pens and materials and felt that these materials served three purposes to help his daughter negotiate the school space. First, he told me that they signaled to the teacher that his daughter was serious about her studies. Second, the possession of these goods showed the teacher that her parents cared about her education. Finally, his daughter would have a positive interaction in school because the teacher would not reprimand or discipline her for not being prepared and presenting sloppy writing. Mr. Lu's observation that his daughter might be reprimanded for not having proper materials showed his understanding of the importance of teacher perceptions in his daughter's schooling experience. Therefore, Mr. Lu armed his daughter with proper pens and school materials so that she could positively negotiate the school environment and made it a positive environment for her to learn, free of teacher criticism. However, most of Mr. Lu's efforts were invisible to the teacher because Lu Xinqi did not bring the good pens to school. Similar to the Hus, Mr. and Mrs. Lu have had educational experiences, which influenced their dispositions and understanding of the educational field. Both families understood the importance that teacher's played in a student's life, and by equipping their children with proper resources, they wanted to convert their invisible labor and capital into a learning resource that would be visible and appreciated by teachers.

Relationship between work and children's learning

All families in my study are farmers; however, to keep up with the costs of education, many families have taken to off-farm work.[1] To support their children's education and provide for the family, Mr. and Mrs. Ya both worked outside the home doing off-farm work. Mrs. Ya told me:

> My husband works as a laborer to earn money. I stay at home to "pull up" (拉扯) the three children. . . . I raised the children until they were school-aged, then I also work as a day laborer.[2] When I work, I rise early [and go to sleep late]. I also make sure that the children are fed, so my working does not impact the issue of them being fed.

Mr. and Mrs. Ya worked additional jobs to support their children's education. It was common to see parents rise around 5 o'clock in the morning to prepare food for their children before they left for their off-farm jobs and returned in the evening. Children would arrive home from school to empty homes. It was important to Mrs. Ya that her children were properly fed so that they could be alert and focused in school. However, Mrs. Ya noted that although working provided resources for her children, it also detracted from their learning as well:

> However, working as a day laborer all day does affect the children. I don't have time to help them with homework. When I return home at night I make dinner and after we eat I am very tired. Therefore, I just want to rest for a

little while. When they [children] ask me questions, I am annoyed, but when I am not annoyed I teach and explain things to them. Mostly, I am the one who teaches them. My husband does not teach them.

Mrs. Ya was unique in that she could help her children with their homework, but because she had to work, she was not able to help her children with their homework. Mrs. Ya told me she was certain that working long hours took away from her capacity to help her children with their schoolwork, which she also saw as important. Moreover, Mrs. Ya admitted that she was tired at the end of a long day of physical labor and had less patience for her children's questions. As a result, making this decision to work longer hours was an important piece of how parents are involved in their children's schooling. Parents were determined to work long hours so that they could purchase learning materials for their children.

Mr. and Mrs. Ya lamented that the school had recently requested that they pay another school fee in recognition of their youngest son. The school planned to hang large posters with pictures of the outstanding students all along the exterior of the school building. Alongside the student pictures would be background information of each student to inspire other students. Mr. and Mrs. Ya were proud of their youngest son for being recognized as an outstanding student in the school. The honor, however, was not free. Mrs. Ya explained:

> To be acknowledged as an outstanding student and then asked to give money, it is not reasonable of the school to ask us to give money. Our economic circumstances are quite difficult, but I think for the sake of the children, for their reputation, I will just give them [the school] the money. 30 *Yuan* is not a big deal. We can simply earn more.

Mr. and Mrs. Ya felt that they could not win – they had to pay additional school fees, even when their children were doing well in school. However, the Yas commitment to their children's education was paramount, even in the face of difficult economic conditions. Almost all of the rural parents with whom I worked echoed this willingness to participate in any type of labor to earn money to provide additional support for their children's schooling.

Mr. Gao, Gao Ling's father, also underscored the necessity to work additional off-farm jobs but also the impact of the work on their children's schooling. Mr. Gao told me, "We go in the morning and return in the evening, we don't work jobs that are far away." Mr. Gao emphasized that it was important to not work too far away from home so that the children could be fed and looked after when they were at home. He went on to echo Mrs. Ya's words:

> Of course our working has an impact on their studies. If we return late, the children won't eat on time, and they love to play and don't complete their homework, we can't supervise them. We will eat late and all we want to do is to sleep. The children are also tired.

Having parents working late influences the meal times as well as parent energy to supervise homework and student energy levels to focus on their homework. Parental willingness to work additional hours or jobs in order to provide financial and physical resources for their children's schooling was a form of involvement that was invisible to teachers. Teachers could not see the physical, mental, and emotional stresses that parents endured so that they could support their children's schooling.

Spring to mid-summer is scorpion-catching season in the area. From about mid-May through July, more than half of the rural parents with whom I worked participated in scorpion-catching as a form of off-farm labor. At 4 o'clock in the afternoon, the main intersection in Zhengxing would be lined with several large trucks. Rural residents piled into the back of the trucks and are whisked away to the deserts in Inner Mongolia and in Ningxia. Each person carried a large flashlight-type light, scarves, homemade wooden tongs, and plastic one-liter soda bottles. Rural residents told me that the ride to the desert usually lasted two to three hours when the ride should have been about an hour because the nearest part of the desert was only about 40 kilometers away. However, road blockades by local officials and residents in the desert communities prolonged the trip for the scorpion catchers. When they finally arrived at the desert, they had to sit and wait for the sun to set as scorpions could only be caught during the night. To protect from the cold and strong winds residents wrapped their shoulders and faces up with the scarves. The light they carried was a black light used to find scorpions and the tongs were used to pick-up the scorpions so that one did not get stung. One had to be quick to catch the scorpions with the tongs and place them in the soda bottles.

In the mornings, when rural residents returned from the desert, they would line the streets holding their plastic bottles of scorpions, waiting to sell them to middlemen. All over the main road, little shops with large red handwritten numbers indicating today's market price for the scorpions popped up overnight. Rural residents were paid according to the total weight of their scorpions. The price for scorpions fluctuated between 75 and 83 *Renminbi* per *jin*[3] during scorpion-catching season. The average amount earned by the rural parents with whom I worked was 28 *Renminbi* a night (vs. 25 *Renminbi* in a day laborer job).[4]

Most parents rushed home by 7 a.m. so that they could prepare breakfast for their children before they left for school and in the afternoon, parents prepared dinner for their children before they left again to catch scorpions. Several rural parents with whom I worked shared with me their rationale for participating in the scorpion-catching. They told me that compared with the other day laborer jobs available in the area, catching scorpions had the potential for better pay. Although scorpion stings were common many rural parents preferred scorpion-catching to less dangerous but also lower paying construction work. Rural parents also preferred the immediate daily compensation scorpion-catching provided as opposed to compensation being given weekly or monthly for day laborer jobs, such as construction, which was paid upon completion of a project. Rural parents risked their health and well-being to catch scorpions in the middle of the night in order to provide additional cash income for the family, some of which was used to purchase children's academic supplies.

Scorpion-catching was an off-farm work that parents engaged in outside of the four farm work cycles. The first cycle begins in March and lasts into May, rural parents are busy preparing the land for planting and for planting of seeds. April and May is consumed with irrigating crops. The second cycle is July and August primarily reaping the summer harvest. The third cycle is the fall harvest in September October. The last cycle is in November/December includes preparing the land for winter. Scorpion-catching season falls in-between the first and second cycles.

As mentioned earlier, teacher perceptions of parental involvement may be related to student achievement (Lee & Bowen, 2006). A study by Yuping Zhang (2008) in rural Gansu investigated how family background influenced children's schooling from a teachers' perspective. Zhang (2008) found that a family's economic situation had no impact on teacher's evaluations and expectations of students. However, teacher perceptions of the student's home cultural environment (measured by illiteracy in the home, parents not caring about schooling, parent ideas of education being different from schools' idea of education, and parents not having a good study plan for their children) was associated with teacher evaluations of the student and expectations for subsequent achievement. Rural parents in Gansu who felt that by providing pens, books, and other schooling materials showed the teacher that they cared about their children's schooling may have merit. Rural parents felt that they could help make the physical school environment a friendly environment for their children when they purchased the best schooling materials for their children. Parents also worked in the home to provide a good learning environment for their children.

A good learning environment: free from financial worry and the importance of continuity in schooling

A good learning environment for parents went beyond the provision of learning materials and included shielding children from the harsh reality of rural poverty and also ensuring continuity of schooling. Every parent repeatedly told me that although they did not have much, it was extremely important not to put their own financial stress on the children. "It is really important for us [Mr. and Mrs. Lu] not to discuss our financial situation in front of the children. It is not good for them to have to worry about money, that is our responsibility," said Mr. Lu. When the children would run off and play in the courtyard or go out with their friends, Mr. Lu would look me sternly in the eyes to tell me that life was very difficult and money was tight. He, Mrs. Lu, and his parents all took on extra paid work so they would have enough for the family. However, when Lu Xinqi would ask her father, "Can I buy a snack today?" without missing a beat Mr. Lu would quickly tell her she could have a snack, even though he did not think they were healthy for her. Mr. Lu turns to me rubbing his head and says, "She needs to eat." Even though the snacks only cost one or two *yuan*, it is money that could go to paying the water bill, buying school supplies, and food.

The financial situation in the Qi home was even more tenuous than the Lu household, and this impacted Qi Youkang. Mrs. Qi told me:

> Sometimes he [Qi Youkang] will say to me, "'Mother, we are so poor.'" I tell him to try his best and study well and if you need to buy something, I will find the money for you. . . . I think that sometimes we put too much pressure on kids. I tell him not to worry about it [not having money]. You only need to complete your schooling; you don't need to be concerned so much [about money]. I ask him why he is so concerned about these things and tell him he should not think too much about them and should just focus on his schooling.

Even though the Qi family did not have very much money, Mrs. Qi tried very hard to shield her son from the burden of worrying about money. She told him that the family would support him financially and that he did not need to worry about it. Furthermore, Qi Youkang's older brother worked outside the home to support his younger brother's education. He sent his work earnings back to the home to support Qi Youkang so he could have the materials he needed for his schooling.

Similar to the Ya and Qi families, Mr. and Mrs. Wen wanted to provide support and resources for their children' schooling. Mr. and Mrs. Wen worked to ensure a good learning environment in terms of providing continuity of schooling for their children. To this end, Mr. and Mrs. Wen told their children that they did not need to worry about financial issues; they simply needed to concentrate on their schooling and do their best. Mr. Wen told me:

> I want them to study as far as they can. . . . I tell them to try their best to learn, I tell them not to give up. . . . I will take care of all the income sources, I don't ask them to take on that burden. I only want them to study well, that is all.

Moreover, Mr. Wen offers a rather graphic description of the level of physical sacrifice he'd be willing to make in order to support them academically. Mr. Wen says, "I say [to them] if I break my skull to support their college education, I must because it is not okay if one of them fails academically." And in his current occupation as a stonecutter, such an injury is one of the hazards of the job. He spent several months home during the study mending an on-the-job injury, a broken foot. Mrs. Wen added, "We hope they will become dragons, if there is a possibility for them to study then I will do anything so that their studies are not interrupted." Mrs. Wen highlighted the importance of continuity in education as a critical component of her children's learning environment. She did not want her children's education interrupted simply because the family could not afford to support it.

Relief from household chores to create a good home environment

As the preceding section highlighted, rural parents supported their children's schooling in their readiness to work extra hours to provide schooling resources for their children. In order to aid their children in their academic endeavors further, rural parents in Gansu showed an overwhelming insistence that their children focus their time on studying instead of participating in household chores. Most of the parents in my sample stressed the importance of having their children focus on their studies. To help their children focus, many rural parents reduced the chores that they expected of their children during the school week. Families differed in their approach to the allocation of chores, but most parents agreed that children should do little to no household work during the school week or school year. Relieving their children of household chores was a large sacrifice by these mothers and fathers, especially because many of these parents also took on additional paid work themselves to support their children's education. In this section, I first present the voices of the families who emphasized the importance of relieving their children of these chores so they could focus their energies on their studies. Similar to parental enthusiasm to take on additional paid work, parents sacrificed their time in order to release children from doing chores was an invisible form of parental involvement to teachers. Then, I present findings from quantitative analyses of the GCSF data that highlight the connection between higher parental educational expectations for their children and the reduction in the child's responsibility for doing household chores.

Mrs. Ao told me that her children should spend their time studying and that she took it upon herself to do the household chores.

> I make every effort so they do not have to do chores, so that they can spend most of their time on their studies. Even if it makes me busier I will do a little here and there when I have free time. Even if I do a little less, no matter what, just as long as my children do a reduced amount of household chores.

However, in light of Mrs. Ao's low educational expectations for her children, her commitment to alleviating her children's chores is surprising because she does not have high educational expectations for academic success. She told me, "I want them [three children] to test into college. But, on the whole, I feel that not one of them will succeed." Mrs. Ao engaged an invisible form of involvement that is important for two reasons; first, she is willing to take on household chores to create an environment for her children to concentrate on their studies and second, Mrs. Ao's dedication to her children's schooling is evident in her willingness to lessen all her children's chores even though she did have not have high educational expectations for her children.

Physically and mentally tiring

Mrs. Yao also relieved her children of doing household chores. Ms. Yao not only worked on off-farm jobs to provide material resources for Xusao's schooling, but also relieved him from doing household chores. Mrs. Yao also felt that her work as a day laborer impacted her children because their dinner meals were sometimes delayed. Echoing Mrs. Gao and Mrs. Ya from earlier in the chapter, many parents spoke of their feelings of guilt if they were late in preparing meals for their children. Mrs. Yao told me:

> I think it means for them to study well, simply to study well. I will do the household chores so they do not need to do them. . . . Sometimes I will work as a day laborer. These days if the children want something and you cannot afford it. . . . If I don't work as a day laborer we won't have any money . . . [and] some places [I work] are up to 10 kilometers away. . . . I come back at night and rush to prepare dinner for the children, it is not good for the children to be hungry, they would starve.

In Mrs. Yao's description, we can see that she not only relieved her children of household chores but also took on outside labor to support their education. Additionally, she rushed home to make sure that her children were fed at night and felt guilty if she were late. The emotional and physical pressure that Mrs. Yao placed upon herself to take on paid labor as well as household duties was invisible to teachers, but was an important support for her children's schooling.

Children are aware of parent sacrifices

Every time I spoke with Mrs. Qi, she pressed upon me the importance of being literate. She repeatedly told me that he (Qi Youkang) needed to write his characters and study well. Mrs. Qi wanted to make sure that he had everything he needed to practice his characters. "By nighttime, I quickly make dinner and tell him to eat quickly and after he's eaten to practice his characters. We strive to have him focus on his studies." Mrs. Qi, who was a day laborer and farmer, told me that she did not ask that her son Qi Youkang do household chores, so that he could focus exclusively on his schooling:

> We don't let him do them [chores], we tell him to study. We don't let him do chores. Anyhow, we don't have many chores, we tell him to study. . . . I always want to make sure he studies, and have never thought of having him do household chores. For the most part, I do the household chores. I don't make him do household chores, but sometimes when he returns home and does not do his homework, I'll ask him if he is lying or did his teacher not assign any homework. When I tell him that I will financially support his schooling, then he'll hurriedly do his homework. Sometimes, it makes me so worried when he tells me that there's nothing he can do, the

information just doesn't stick. We don't have any education, so I feel awful.

We whole-heartedly want them to be successful academically. We make every effort to allow our children to study well. We are busy, we want him to do his homework well, study well, and I will do all the chores.

We can see that Mrs. Qi expected her son to study in his free time. However, based on her limited education and understanding of schoolwork, she was unable to gauge whether or not her son really had homework when he returned from school. As mentioned earlier in this chapter, Qi Youkang expressed his concern over the family's financial situation. Here again, we see that after his mother assured him that they would support him financially, he returned to do his homework.

Although Mrs. Qi relieved Qi Youkang from doing household chores, Qi Youkang was aware of the sacrifices that his parents and brother made on his behalf. During another visit, Mrs. Qi told me:

He does do them [chores]. When he returns from school he will carry water. For the most part, most kids who perform poorly in school do not like to do household chores. When our child returns home he'll first eat a little something and then on his own initiative he will do some household chores. He is very considerate and says to me, "Mom, you rest, let me go fetch the water." After he has carried the water into the house he will do his homework.

Qi Youkang demonstrated that children were not oblivious to the sacrifices that their family made for their schooling. Qi Youkang did what he could to help, including carrying water. Even while acknowledging that Qi Youkang's school performance was poor Mrs. Qi was still willing to support his schooling. Teachers and schools cannot see that Mrs. Qi sacrificed her time to do additional housework so that her academically poor-performing son could focus on his studies.

Children have to think of their parents

Not all parents released their children from all household duties. On several occasions when I visited the Wen household I would find Wen Yijin in the courtyard sitting on a simple wooden stool, shoulders hunched over a large plastic tub of clothing. Wen Yijin would look up and quickly smile and greet me and then return to scrubbing the dirty clothes. After she had scrubbed the clothes she would pour the dirty laundry water on the ground and hang each article of clothing across the small plot of garden in the courtyard.

Mr. Wen told me that he expected his daughter to do light housework. As mentioned above, Mr. Wen wanted both of his children to attend college. But Mr. Wen also felt Wen Yijin should do chores to understand the sacrifices her mother made. Mr. Wen explicitly told Wen Yijin that she had to do some chores because her mother worked hard to support her financially and that Wen Yijin should help her mother. Mr. Wen said:

> For the most part, we don't ask them to do any work, just the household chores. Keep the courtyard clean, and on Sundays my daughter will wash her own clothes. I tell her that she should wash her own clothes and cannot expect her mother to wash her clothes and cook. Her mom also has to go out and work to financially support her education. He emphasizes she has to compare herself to her mother; and after she compares herself to her mother she will know what she must do.

Unlike Mrs. Yao, who tried to shield her son from the reality that relieving her son of chores added to her own burden, Mr. Wen explicitly explained to Wen Yijin that she had to pitch in to help the family in order to understand the sacrifices made by her mother to support her education. On several other occasions, Mr. and Mrs. Wen emphasized that "When we get busy, as peasants there is always a lot of work to do. So, my daughter will have to take care of the meals and take charge of some of the other chores." Mr. Wen underscores the amount of labor that rural parents have to do to maintain the land. Mr. Wen had high educational expectations and still expected his daughter to do chores, unlike Qi Youkang, whose mother alleviated his chores, even though he was a poor-performing student.

Parent educational expectations and household chores

Using data drawn from the GSCF, I investigated whether parents with different educational expectations of their children assigned different amounts of chores. Specifically, I asked do parents with higher educational expectations assign children fewer chores than parents with lower educational expectations? The research site for the quantitative component of my study was the same province as the qualitative component.

Data set and sample

I drew on a unique dataset, obtained using the Gansu Survey of Children and Families (GSCF), which was administered in 2000, 2004, and 2007 to 2,000 children aged 9 to 12 in 20 rural counties in Gansu province (see Figure I.1 in the Introduction). In the GSCF project, a multi-stage cluster sampling process, with stratified random selection within clusters, was used to draw the self-weighting sample of 2,000 children. Questionnaires were administered to mothers, fathers, the target child, the target child's homeroom teacher, school teachers, school principals, and village leaders. For this book, I analyzed the 2004 wave of data because I wanted both the quantitative and qualitative data from the same years, 2004 and 2005. As a GSCF project member, I aided in the survey design of this work, working on the drafting and revision of the mother questionnaire. I developed survey questions based on current conceptions of parental involvement for the mother questionnaire.

Measures

I included outcome, question, and control variables in my analyses. First, I created a dichotomous outcome variable, ANYCHORE, that records the child's self-report of whether he or she did daily chores at home (1 = did chores and 0 = did not do chores). My one principal question predictor, MOTHEREXP, is a categorical variable that describes the mother's educational expectation for her child. To represent this predictor in my analyses, I converted it into a vector of dichotomous variables representing each level of the mother's educational expectation, primary, middle school, high school, college, and other. As is usual in these types of analyses, I control for selected demographic variables, including the child's age in years (AGE), the number of children in the family (NKIDS, continuous variable), whether the target child is female (SEX, coded as 1 for female and 0 for male) family wealth (WEALTH a continuous variable), mother's education (MED, continuous variable of each year of education), and father's education (FED, continuous variable of each year of education) (Gomes, 1984; Pong, 1997). Additionally, in terms of allocation of chores to the child, I also included covariates to describe whether the mother was present in the home (MOMHOME, coded as 1 if she was in the home and 0 otherwise), whether the father was present in the home (DADHOME, coded as 1 if he was in the home and 0 otherwise), and the parents' perception of their child's health compared to other children in the village (WELLCHILD, coded as 1 = not very good, 2 = not good, 3 = average, 4 = good, and 5 = very good). I also included village fixed effects in my statistical models to account for the clustering of kids within villages, and consequently, investigated only the variation within village.

Data analysis

I used binomial logistic regression analysis to address my research question which asked – Do parents with higher educational expectations assign children fewer chores than parents with lower educational expectations? In my analyses, in addition to the usual covariates, I controlled for the fixed effects of village to account for the unobserved effects of the clustering of children and families within villages, on my outcome. A typical statistical model is:

$$p(ANYCHORE_{ic}=1) = \frac{1}{1+e^{-(\beta_{0c}+\beta_1 MOTHEREXP_{ic}+\gamma'Z)}},$$

where β_{0c} represents the community-specific fixed effect (intercept) of village c, and β_1 is a parameter that represents the impact of the mother's educational

88 Active rural parents' hidden work

Table 5.1 Summary statistics for selected variables

	Mean	Standard Deviation	Minimum	Maximum
Outcome variable				
Chore status ($n = 1{,}948$)	0.29	0.46	0	1
Predictor variable				
Primary school graduate Expectation ($n = 1{,}863$)	0.01	0.08	0	1
Middle school graduate expectation ($n = 1{,}863$)	0.13	0.34	0	1
High school graduate expectation ($n\text{--} = 863$)	0.34	0.47	0	1
College or beyond graduate expectation ($n = 1{,}863$)	0.34	0.48	0	1
Other expectation ($n = 1{,}863$)	0.01	0.09	0	1
Control variables				
Mother's education level ($n = 1{,}863$)	4.32	3.45	0	13
Father's education level ($n = 1{,}864$)	7.12	3.64	0	29
Number of kids in the family ($n = 1{,}865$)	2.33	0.72	1	6
Family wealth ($n = 1{,}865$)	10,649.29	36,247.48	120	974,900
Child's age ($n = 1{,}864$)	15.08	1.16	12	20
Mother in the home ($n = 1{,}863$)	0.98	0.16	0	1
Father in the home ($n = 1{,}864$)	0.78	0.41	0	1
Child's health ($n = 1{,}863$)	4.09	0.93	1	5

Source: GSCF-2 Mother, Child, and Household questionnaires.

expectations on whether child i in community c is asked to perform chores, controlling for covariates Z. If parameter β_1 is statistically significant and negative, then I conclude that parents with higher expectations assign fewer chores to their children.

In Table 5.1, I present descriptive statistics on selected variables from my quantitative analysis. On my principal dichotomous question variable of whether children did chores, the sample average was .29, indicating that more than 70% of children did not do chores. On average, parents believed that their children would graduate from high school (sample average = .34). In Table 5.2, exploratory contingency table analyses suggest that children of parents who had educational expectations for them of junior high school ($\chi^2 = 8.43$; $p < .01$), high school ($\chi^2 = 2.98$; $p < .1$), or college and beyond ($\chi^2 = 7.59$; $p < .01$) did indeed spend less time doing chores.

This same relationship was also evident in the village fixed effects logistic regression analyses presented in Table 5.3. The fitted odds that a student whose

Table 5.2 Parental educational expectations and child chore status

	Child chore status		
	Child does not do chores	Child does chores	χ^2
	n = 1378	n = 570	
Parental educational expectations			
Primary school	58.33	41.67	0.09
Junior high school	62.9	37.1	8.43**
High school	73.26	29.26	2.98~
College and beyond	74.54	25.46	7.59**
Other	46.67	53.33	4.23*

Source: GSCF-2 Child and Household questionnaires.

~$p < .1$. *$p < .05$. **$p < .01$.

Table 5.3 Parameter estimates (and standard errors and p values) for a taxonomy of logistic regression models for parental educational expectations and child chore status, controlling for background characteristics

	Fixed effect #1		SE	Fixed effect #2		SE
Predictor variable						
Mother's educational expectations						
Primary school graduate	0.22		−0.63	0.25		0.64
Middle school graduate	0.19		0.2	0.01		0.2
High school graduate	−0.35	*	0.16	−0.36	*	0.16
College and beyond graduate	−0.43	*	0.17	−0.44	**	0.17
Other	0.44		0.55	0.52		0.56
Control variables						
Family wealth				0	~	0
Mother's education level				0.03		0.02
Father's education level				0.01		0.02
Number of children in the family				0.04		0.08
Child age				−0.04		0.05
Gender				−0.04		0.11
Mother in the home				−0.17		0.34
Father in the home				−0.13		0.14
Child health status				−0.03		0.06
Log likelihood	−867.38			863.19		
N	1,842			1,842		

Source: GSCF-2 Mother, Child and Household questionnaires.

~$p < .1$. *$p < .05$. **$p < .01$.

parents expected them to graduate from middle school would do chores were 1.01 times the odds for students whose parents had other educational expectations. The fitted odds that a student whose parents expected them to graduate from high school would do chores were .70 times the odds for students whose parents had other educational expectations for that student. The fitted odds for a student whose parents expected them to graduate from college or beyond would do chores were .64 times the odds for students whose parents had other educational expectations. Thus, students whose parents had expectations that they would complete high school or above were less likely to do chores.

Conclusion

In this chapter, we see that rural parents were willing to endure hardship so that their children could have greater educational opportunities. They took on additional jobs to earn money to provide schooling materials and to pay for tutoring, an additional year of schooling, and other school expenses. Rural parents provided their children with schooling materials to aid their learning. By relieving children of chores parents also take on additional work inside the home. This willingness to take on additional work both in and out of the home, demonstrated that rural parents are serious about their schooling. Data from the GSCF also shows that rural parents with higher educational expectations of their children assigned their children fewer chores.

Rural parents viewed the provision of financial support and schooling resources as a tangible support for their children's schooling that made their children's schooling experience better. Rural parents with whom I worked believed that material resources were an important part of providing a good learning environment for their children in the home and at school. As mentioned earlier in this book, poor rural parents felt limited in their ability to help their children academically in terms of reviewing homework, providing academic stimulation, or going to talk with teachers. As discussed in Chapter 4, most rural parents supported their children's own agency in the school space. Many rural parents identified having the proper pens and books as essential to the teachers treating their child seriously in school. This invisible strategy of working off-farm and taking on household chores to equip their children with new and proper schooling materials and time to study demonstrates parental involvement in their children's schooling.

Notes

1 Opportunities for off-farm work have increased since decollectivization occurred in the 1980s. Families were allocated smaller plots of land based on household size.
2 Many of the jobs that parents participated in were related to road construction. Road expansion in rural areas promoted local economies and incomes (Qiao, Rozelle, Huang, Zhang, & Luo, 2014).
3 A *jin* is a Chinese catty, or Chinese pound. It is roughly 500g.
4 The scorpions were sold to medicine makers in South China to make herbal remedies from the scorpion's poison.

6 Information network
Support of family and friends

As I crested the dusty slope that led into Le Xin village, I noticed several villagers clustered together along the right side of the road. At first, I thought they were all huddled together looking at household wares being sold by a peddler. As I walked closer, I could overhear bits of the conversation: "The Wang child is ranked first in her class" "Do you know who is ranked first in the other class?" Chinese educational policies have been enacted to banish the use of class rankings at the primary school level. However, rural parents still use class rankings as an indicator of their children's success in the educational system. What I found quite interesting was how parents, neighbors, friends, and relatives learned of examination results and how they exchanged academic information to support their children's schooling.

The Wus talked with neighbors about student grades and had kin in the schools. During several of my interviews with rural parents, their friends, relatives, or neighbors would be present. It was commonplace in this community for rural residents to just "drop by" (串门)at the homes of relatives, friends, and neighbors without prior notice. One afternoon, while I was chatting with Mrs. Wu, her neighbor, Mrs. Yu, dropped by and added her views on how parents gathered information about their children's schooling. Rural residents were comfortable chatting with friends and neighbors about their children's schooling and turned to their friends and neighbors when they had academic questions. When I probed into how parents learned about their children's achievement, Mrs. Yu told me that "parents look up test scores." I asked her how she looked up test scores, and she responded, matter-of-factly, "Parents all chat about test scores." Mrs. Wu immediately nodded, smiled, and agreed with Mrs. Yu's response and said, "We all chat." After midterm examinations or final examinations, it was not uncommon to hear parents talking with one another about their children's test scores. In fact, most of the parents in my study could tell me which kids scored the highest on the examinations. Not only did rural residents chat with other parents, but Mrs. Wu and Mrs. Yu also shared with me that they often just asked children they met on the street about their test results. Similarly, Yao Xusao's mother told me that she listened to others talking about children's test results but was embarrassed by her son's performance, and therefore she "doesn't dare to chat" with adults about test results. Instead, she asked kids in the neighborhood about their test scores.

Rural parents engaged in the invisible form of involvement as they actively sought out academic and school-related information within their social networks to help their children's schooling. There were two main social interactions in which rural parents engaged to exchange academic information. First, rural parents drew on their networks of school classmates and production brigade teammates. Second, rural parents chatted with relatives, neighbors, and friends. Parents actively gathered four types of academic information, general information about school performance, academic support for homework or examinations, academic role models, and educational opportunities.

It is important to note that rural parents are a part of many social networks, and that by presenting this topography of social interactions to describe how rural parents drew on their social networks to support their children's schooling, I do not mean to define their social networks as fitting into rigid categories. In fact, many of the social networks of the rural parents overlapped. For example, a father was classmates with the principal of the school while the mother was a cousin of the teacher. The information gathered from these overlapping networks varied across rural parents, but the rural parents were the most comfortable tapping into those networks that were already established. By this, I mean that most rural parents turned to their social networks for information and support rather than going to the school to meet with the teachers.

Rural parents engaged in social interactions that drew on their social networks *guanxi* (关系). In Yan Yunxiang's (1996) study of rural social networks and reciprocity, he laid out a structure of how *guanxi* networks are structured in the village of Xiajia. Yan found that community solidarity and familial support was preserved through kinship and non-kinship ties. Yan (1996) observed that a new form of connectedness emerged after collectivization that tied all members of production teams together and turned community ties into personal ties. Using Yan's description of non-kin and kinship networks, I found that parents with whom I worked were most comfortable interacting with their preexisting non-kin and kinship relationships.

As I discussed earlier, few rural parents chose visible forms of involvement by going directly to the schools to gather information about their children's schooling. Formally, teachers would invite parents to the school for parent–teacher meetings and for individual meetings. During my fieldwork, there was not one parent–teacher conference held in either sixth-grade classroom. I did observe parent–teacher conference meetings at other grade levels. As many parents discussed earlier, teachers would invite parents to school, but parents often did not accept the invitation because like Mr. Wu, their children did not pass on the message or like Mrs. Qi, parents felt they were uneducated and therefore would not go to the schools. Instead, they tended to speak with neighbors, including children, kinfolk in the village, and friends, about children's academic achievement and school issues.

The few rural parents in my study who visited the school went to chat with teachers who were their schoolmates, friends, or family members. Their visits to the school were social visits more than professional visits intended to improve parent–teacher relations. In the context of visiting their friends and relatives, rural parents gathered bits of information about the school and the student population. Most of these interactions were usually social visits and, as such, rural parents could casually gather information about their children's schooling. In this chapter, through the narratives of six families we learn how parents seek out school information, homework help, successful family members, and educational opportunities for their children.

General academic information

As I walked up to the primary school, I had to be careful to make my way past the sea of bicycles, a small car, and a pick-up truck, all parked outside the school gate. It was a special day: it was Children's Day and was being celebrated with a morning program in the schoolyard that showcased students from all grades dancing, singing, and performing martial arts. When I arrived, children were already performing and parents, teachers, and other villagers were watching the children in awe. After the morning show, I noticed that Mr. Wen, Wen Yijin's father, was in attendance, and I walked over to him. Mr. Wen and I exchanged pleasantries and made our way over to Principal Xu's office. As I entered Mr. Xu's office, I saw that there are two male teachers (one current and one retired) sitting on the couch. When Mr. Wen entered the office, Mr. Xu pretended to shoo Mr. Wen out of the door. Mr. Xu and Mr. Wen laughed and then filed into the office. Later, Mr. Chi, the accountant, also joined us. The men began smoking and chatting about how rural parents value activities like today's Children's Day performances. They commented on the great turnout for the day's event. Then, they discussed some of the technical difficulties that occurred, including several microphone failures and speaker silences. After about 10 minutes, the men filed out of the office. After they had have left, Mr. Xu told me that he and Mr. Wen were schoolmates and that he often came by to ask how his daughter was doing in school. Mr. Xu looked at me and shook his head, saying "If he [Mr. Wen] wants to know how she is doing then he should go talk to her teacher."

Mr. Xu's description of his chats with Mr. Wen indicated that Mr. Wen was interested in his daughter's education and illustrated his drawing on his preexisting relationship with Mr. Xu to gather information about her education. Mr. Wen told me that he often went to the school because "the primary school principal is my classmate and the middle school principal is in my age-cohort. . . . We'll [parents] go to communicate about our children's schooling." He told me that "Xu Shihen [principal] and I are classmates and I sometimes drop by and chat for a little bit, to understand how my daughter is doing."

Through his preexisting relationship with Mr. Xu and Mr. She (the middle school principal), Mr. Wen sought to find out about his children's academic environment so that he could support their education. Mr. Wen engaged in chats with his schoolmate, Mr. Xu, but had limited interactions with the teachers. Mr. Wen knew that Wen Yijin had a new *banzhuren* but had not met her. Even though his efforts were not successful because the principal did not have information about the day-to-day progress of his children, Mr. Wen's efforts showed that he was interested and drew on his social network to support his children's schooling. Mr. Wen was leveraging his social resources to find out about his daughter's schooling, but was not getting the information he sought. He was physically visible in the school however his interactions were invisible to his daughter's teacher.

When I was chatting with Mr. Wu about his knowledge of the school and staff I learned that Mr. Wu knew Principal Xu. When I asked Mr. Wu how he knew Principal Xu he told me, "He is from our area around here, he is one of us." Mr. Wu had only attended two years of schooling and could have been a classmate of Principal Xu's, but Mr. Wu explained to me that Principal Xu was a member of the local community. He felt comfortable with Principal Xu, even though he was more educated and the principal, but he was familiar because he was from the area. Mr. Wu told me of a recent meeting with Principal Xu to discuss his son's academic standing:

> The principal told us to think about it. If we wanted him to continue he could continue. That he [son] was already 14 almost 15 years old and you [Mr. Wu] still want to keep him in primary school. In second and third grade I asked the principal to watch over him and he told me to talk with the homeroom teacher. I said to him, "You accept the tuition money, even when the school quality is still so poor. Taking in 300–400 *Renminbi* per primary school student."

Mr. Wu was often concerned about money and the high cost of sending both of his sons to school. On top of that, Mr. Wu had concerns about the quality of schooling his children received. As discussed earlier, Mr. Wu felt that Wu Zimou's basic foundations were lacking, resulting in his current poor performance. Mr. Wu was concerned about Wu Zimou repeating and being one of the oldest students in the grade. Similar to Mr. Wen, Principal Xu suggested that Mr. Wu speak directly to the teacher to gain a better understanding of his son's schooling.

Chang Bao was one of the youngest children in his class and was an average student. He was an only child and the only singleton in the families that I interviewed. His father, Mr. Chang, had completed middle school and his mother had completed primary school. Chang Bao's family lived at the edge of town, right off the main road, near the northern gas station (only two gas stations in town). The family had seven *mu* of land. In addition to farming the land, the Chang family was in the pig farming business. The Chang family bought pigs and raised piglets,[1] which they sold for a profit (see Figure 6.1). Mr. Chang told me that he could sell a healthy one-month old piglet for 180 *Yuan*.[2] When I entered their yard, to my left were three pig pens and to my right, one small building. The Chang family did not have a garden in the yard but did have one outside the yard where they planted fruits and vegetables for their own consumption.

Both Mr. Wen and Mr. Chang physically visited schools, which I consider visible involvement; however, both fathers preferred to engage in forms of involvement that were largely invisible to their children's teachers. Chang Bao's father also knew the principal of Zhengxing primary school because they were

Support of family and friends 95

Figure 6.1 Pig

from the same village. They attended school around the same time; the principal being just two years ahead of Mr. Chang. They had also worked in the same work unit (production brigade). In Mr. Chang's explanation of why he visited the school the last couple of times, we observe his comfort level with the principal:

> I've been to school twice, this year I've gone to the school less than in previous years. This year the school didn't call on us parents. He [Chang Bao] completes his homework on time, anyway, this year I haven't been called on [by the teacher]. In third grade, oh we went! The number of times I visited the school was so many that I didn't have the face to go in the classroom. I told him this, as soon as I entered the school ground, the students would say, "Chang Bao's father is here, it is probably because he [Chang Bao] did not turn in his homework"... I went down to the school to chat with the principal, I did not meet with the teacher, I just chatted with the principal.

On another occasion, when Chang Bao was not doing his homework, Mr. Chang again went to chat with the principal. Mr. Chang told me:

> The principal told me that I know a little and I should go to communicate with the teachers to understand Chang Bao's schooling situation ... try to find some time to go the school.

Mr. Chang consistently visited the school to chat with the principal. Mr. Chang also knew Chang Bao's *banzhuren* (homeroom teacher) because they had worked on the same production brigade. Mr. Chang explained to me how he knew Mrs. Gu:

> She [Mrs. Gu] used to teach at Boqi primary school, I know her. She was in my production brigade, [we were] in the same production team. So, I already know her, I know that she was teaching in Boqi. At the start of this year, Chang Bao told me that his *banzhuren* is Gu Jufou, then I knew that she was transferred to this school. Since I already knew her, I was clear about who she is. I do not know who his math or English teachers are.

During my initial discussion with Mrs. Gu about families that she considered involved, she mentioned Chang Bao's family. Mrs. Gu and I sat down in her office reviewing the midterm examinations. She told me that Mr. Chang was one of the few parents who wrote something on the comment portion of midterm examination. Teachers usually had students take their midterm examination paper home to have their parents examine their work and requested that parents send feedback to the teachers on the back of the midterm examination. In his comment about the exam, Mr. Chang shared with Mrs. Gu that Chang Bao liked to play at home and wondered what he was like in school. Mr. Chang also wrote that Chang Bao was not studious and viewed doing homework as completing a task. Mrs. Gu noted that the Chang family *bijiao zhongshi* (placed more value on) Chang Bao's schooling than other families.

Mrs. Gu confirmed that parents sent feedback to teachers after exams, "usually after the tests . . . we ask the parents to sign [and provide feedback on] the tests. The most requested comment by [parents] is to have teachers teach more." Mrs. Gu told me Mr. Chang's comment on the exam:

> In the home, children do not focus on their studies, they like to play, they don't put their thoughts on studying. [We] don't know what their attitudes are like in school. These types of questions, what are the attitudes of students in the school, since they have these questions, parents should interact with teachers and communicate.

Mr. Chang's efforts to gather information about his son's schooling attitudes was visible to Mrs. Gu, however, she echoed the principal, Mr. Xu's comment that parents should come to the school and talk with the teachers to understand their children's academic life.

When I shared some initial finding that parents were either unaware that they were invited to the school because they never received the invitation or that parents were uncomfortable meeting her, the teacher, Mrs. Gu paused and reflected:

> I think that as a *banzhuren* I have not fully done my job, we should know the family situation of our students. As a teacher, we should pay at least one visit

to student homes to meet with the parents. But, I've never done that. That is to say I haven't fully done my job.

Mrs. Gu was aware that understanding the home situation of her students was important, however, she did not have time to visit the homes of her students. When I started my research, Mrs. Gu confidently told me that she was a rural parent and understood the life of a farmer and that farmers are busy and only concerned with their work.

Role models and encouragement

Zhu Hanqi was 13 years old and a high-performing student. He had an older sister, Zhu Yuqin, 15 years old and in seventh grade. Hanqi lived with his parents and grandmother in a one-room cement house behind their family restaurant. The restaurant was located on a main road that passes through the town. They have owned the restaurant for over 11 years. Mr. Zhu grew up in the village where they currently reside, and both parents attended the local primary school in their area. Mrs. Zhu completed third grade and Mr. Zhu completed fifth grade. For a family of five, they owned five *mu* of land.

Mr. and Mrs. Zhu and I sat in one of the back rooms of the restaurant discussing the recent midterm exams. Hanqi did well on the examinations and is being rewarded with a visit to his grandmother's house in the village. I asked Mr. and Mrs. Zhu who they talked to about their children's schooling, Mr. Zhu immediately said, "The principal and not the teachers because the principal and I were classmates and attended the same primary school together." Similar to Mr. Wen and Mr. Chang, Mr. Zhu explained that the principal as most appropriate person to chat with at school because they had a long history together and were old friends.

Mr. and Mrs. Zhu were very proud of their son's performance, and Mr. Zhu offered his explanation as to why his children had good study habits and excelled in school. Mr. Zhu sat up straight and his body rocked back and looked me in the eye and said, "Our nieces and nephews have passed the college entrance examination and now have proper jobs. Having nieces and nephews that were successful have helped shape the studying success phenomenon in the family." Mr. Zhu let's out a sigh as he shares that he and his siblings are uneducated. Mr. Zhu says that he is close with his siblings, nieces, and nephews and sees them often or talks on the telephone. Mrs. Zhu smiles and chimes in and says that she may not be educated so she cannot answer homework questions, but her children have cousins they can call up for help. Having family members who were educated served as examples of educational success but also resources for being successful in the educational system through good study habits and provision of tutoring help.

In sharing with me his job experiences, Mr. Wen revealed the important role that kinship ties played in his life. Mr. Wen obtained most the leads for many of his previous temporary jobs from family members. In addition to job information, Mr. Wen also learned how essential education was to gainful employment. Similar to other rural parents, he told me that he could see that those who had been educated had an easier time of finding employment and that even with his educational experiences he had been turned away from several positions. In Mr. Wen's description of how his relatives encouraged him to support his children's education, we can see that Mr. Wen received encouragement from family to support his children's schooling.

Both Mr. and Mrs. Wen had family members who had been academically successful. At family get-togethers, Mr. Wen chatted with them about his children's education. He recounted a recent visit to me:

> My brother-in-law, his wife, and my cousin all have done well in school. . . . Every year they come to our house and say that I should monitor my children's schooling and emphasize that I should not give it a pass. [They tell him] "If they can study, it is good for them and good for you. So, you have to say nice things. . . . So if they are able to study, I will do everything in my power to allow that to happen."

Mr. Wen was comfortable interacting with his family members and valued the advice he received from them. These interactions reinforced the importance of education for his children's future, and specifically the important role that parents played in supporting their education. As discussed in Chapter 2, rural parents viewed education as important for participation in the modern economy and for gaining entry into the urban lifestyle. Family and friends were a great source of encouragement for rural parents as they strove to support their children's schooling. Mr. Wen's father often told him:

> We are not educated, [you] must use all your efforts to support your children's schooling. . . . Staying in these areas, there are few rural opportunities . . . nowadays, things are all mechanized . . . I feel that they should study as much as they can possibly study. I hope they will be able to be successful, that's it.

The Wen family echoes how many rural families see the future opportunities available to their children in rural areas as being very limited. They also reflect on the limitations of their own educational background as support for more schooling opportunities for their children.

Rural parents interacted with their kin in the city to learn about what was happening in schools and how urban parents supported their children's education. Many rural parents with family and friends in the city would refer to the types of support that urban parents provided. Mr. Lu told me:

> I see that parents in the city really care about their children's schooling. They hire tutors to come to their home and on the weekends they have their children go to review/tutoring classes. . . . I see this in Junxi (the city) in the homes of my relatives, they all do these things. Parents really care and do a lot for their children's schooling.

Mr. Lu was comfortable talking to his family and learning about how they supported their children's schooling. By accessing family who lived in the city, Mr. Lu saw the types of parental support that were absent in the rural areas. I argue that Mr. Lu's social interactions with his urban relatives actually provided a strategy that he used to expand his own expectations for his children and served to help him support their schooling. His interactions with his urban relatives and friends helped him understand more about the provision of tutoring.

Even though there were no tutors in the rural areas, Mr. Lu still found ways to support his children's schooling. When he could not answer all of his daughter's homework questions, Mr. Lu suggested that she, "ask the older middle school students in the village." He recommended that she "seek out those middle school students who have time and ask them." By suggesting that his daughter seeks help from middle school students in the village Mr. Lu demonstrated his inclination to turn towards fellow villagers for help and that he was comfortable with them. Unlike urban parents who could hire tutors, Mr. Lu drew on the resources in the village, mainly the more educated youth.

As discussed in Chapter 4, most rural parents expected their children to take responsibility for their own learning. Notice that Mr. Lu did not interact personally with the middle school students on behalf of his daughter, he expected her to take responsibility for her own education and obtain the help that she needed. While he did not intervene on her behalf, he did offer suggestions on how to access help, which made the academic environment pleasant. Also, Mr. Lu's suggestion to Lu Xingqi that she turn to the other villagers for help set an example of how fellow villagers could be sources of support. Similarly, Mrs. Zhu does not mediate the relationship between her children and nieces and nephews. Mrs. Zhu tells her children that they can pick up the phone and call their cousins for educational support.

Academic help

Mr. Wu also used an invisible form of parental involvement when he drew upon his kinship relationship to keep abreast of how his older son, Wu Duxi, was doing in school. Mr. Wu's uncle taught in the middle school. Mr. Wu did not go to the school to talk with his son's teachers but knew that his son was not studious in class. When I asked Mr. Wu how he knew this, and he told me:

> I have a relative who is there with him [in school].... My uncle, Wu Maoqi....
> I tell him [son, Wu Duxi] that if he doesn't understand something to go ask his great-uncle. He [great-uncle] is educated, he is a teacher and he will be able to teach you. If there's anything you don't know go ask your great-uncle. Don't be scared.

Mr. Wu's strategy for helping his oldest son was to connect Wu Duxi with his great-uncle. Additionally, he gathered information about how his son was doing from his uncle, for example, that Wu Duxi was not studious in class. Mr. Wu did not go to the school himself but drew on his kinship ties to understand his son's behavior and achievement in school. In this example, we again see the Mr. Wu believed that his son took on the responsibility for his own schooling and must seek help when he needed it. Mr. Wu simply offered up the resources he had available in order to make Wu Duxi's schooling experience more positive. Mr. Wu noted that when his great uncle would visit, his sons were too scared to talk to him. Mr. Wu said, "They don't dare say a word. They need help, but suddenly they can't remember anything anymore." Moreover, Mr. Wu was not inclined to visit the middle school, but was more comfortable communicating with his uncle about his son's schooling. Similarly, Gao Ling's family also turned to family and relatives for academic help. Mr. Gao told me, "If they don't know how to do the homework, parents have to be patient and cannot say we can't coach them so they just give up and don't do it. Even if they don't know how to do it, they have to look at each one and they could also ask their cousin." Many parents had at least one extended family member who had completed more schooling than they themselves had and would turn to family members for help.

Educational opportunities

In July, at the end of the school year, I entered the Ao family shop to find Mrs. Ao anxiously pacing about the shop. She was on the telephone when I entered and invited me to sit in the back of the store. I knew something was on her mind, but could not figure it out. While we were chatting about her children's final examination results and about summer tutoring, Mrs. Ao revealed to me that her older daughter scored just below the minimum high school examination score and that she was in a quandary about what to do next. We spent the rest of our meeting talking about what to do about Ao Qihui's predicament. Mrs. Ao told me:

> I have been under a lot of pressure these last few days, especially today. I've been in a sticky situation all day, to let her go on or not let her go on. If she goes onto [to high school], she scored 40 points less [she scored 506 and needed 554], I'm afraid that that she [Ao Qihui] will not be able to keep up. On the other hand, I am afraid that if she repeats and studies again, she still might not gain entrance [to high school]. I feel so very anxious . . . I have asked a relative of mine to come this afternoon and get her on the limited list [list of students who did not make the high school cut-off score, but still enter high school]. In my opinion, she is still young, she could repeat another year and see if she tests into high school on her own, then she will study well. She [Ao Qihui] does not want to just sit around, she does not want to repeat. She doesn't want to face her teachers and friends. . . . I haven't spoken to the teachers, I didn't go to the school. When the examinations were done I wanted to go talk to her *banzhuren* to ask if having her repeat was a good idea, but I was in such a quandary that I didn't end up going to the school.

Mrs. Ao then proceeded to tell me about the high school options:

> Hua Jing High School is a new school and I don't know anything about it. I want her to go to the Number Two High School,[3] but we don't have any relatives there, the cut-off for the Number Two High School is too high, therefore Number One High School it is. We have a relative there so we'll go to the Number One High School. . . . People say that the Number Two High School is a better school. . . . The two of us [Mr. and Mrs. Ao] are not educated so we know nothing about this aspect of schooling all we know is that she [Ao Qihui] wants to continue studying. I am in such a jam, I asked my daughter again and she definitely will not repeat the grade. I don't have any choice – I will have to spend the money to support her education, if she gets in.

Our discussion was cut short when her husband and daughter rushed into the shop. Mrs. Ao tells Ao Qihui to quickly brush her hair and wash her face because their relative was going to come meet her and take her to the city to meet with people about the Number One High School.

This example illustrates two strategies that parents in my sample used to support their children's education. First, Mrs. Ao believed that her daughter should take responsibility for her own learning and even make her own decisions regarding whether to repeat a year of school. While Mrs. Ao wanted her daughter to succeed in school and was concerned that her daughter would struggle when she went to high school the following year, she left the decision to repeat the year with Ao Qihui. Notably, Ao Qihui's decision has consequences for the family: Ao Qihui will have to live with relatives to attend high school should she decide not to repeat ninth grade.

Second, this example also demonstrates how parents with whom I worked also used familial networks in order to obtain information about school quality and even to enroll their children in schools. While Mrs. Ao wanted to consult with Ao Qihui's teacher, Ms. Ao was not comfortable talking with the teacher and was unsure about how she would start the conversation. So, in the end, Mrs. Ao relied on her kinship ties to try to gain Ao Qihui entry into high school. The use of these *guanxi* networks resonated with previous parental involvement research. Both Pena (2001) and Lareau (2003) found that working-class families had an intense kinship network, and that working-class and poor parents spent much of their free time with their families. Middle-class families, by comparison, engaged in "concerted cultivation," where they sought out new relationships with the parents of their children's friends and classmates (Lareau, 2003). Middle-class families also differed from the poor and working-class families in that the wealthier families had informal relationships ties to educators.

Families in my study, like Lareau's (2003) working-class and poor families, relied on their kinship networks information and support. Rural parents in my study, like Lareau's families, used their preexisting kinship networks as a source of information about their children's experience in school. Poor families in my study differed from families in Lareau's study, however, in that parents in my study counted school administrators and teachers among the friends and relatives in their social networks, comparable to the ties that Lareau's middle-class families' informal ties to educators.

Rural parents with whom I worked, in contrast to families in Lareau's study, did not make a concerted effort to cultivate relationships with other parents. Most rural parents asked around the village with neighbors or neighborhood children about test grades, but did nothing beyond that in terms of gathering daily information about school or teaching/learning skills. In fact, many parents knew their children's friends, but did not know the parents. Rural parents turned to their preexisting social networks as informal conduits for academic information and support to help their children's schooling.

Conclusion

As discussed in Chapter 2, rural parents in Gansu felt that their position in society was lower than that of teachers. However, when parents engaged with their peers, their social position did not appear to limit their interactions with school personnel. Rural parents in my study preferred to seek out with people with whom they felt most comfortable and through preexisting networks, even the school principal. In the hierarchy of the school, principals were seen as being more senior and it would seem that parents would be more fearful of interacting with principals than with teachers. However, my findings indicate that rural parents interacted with people with whom they were most familiar and comfortable, regardless of position. It is interesting to note that rural parents in my study go to the schools visibly to talk with the principal, but this type of involvement is invisible to their child's teacher. Similarly, family interactions were invisible to teachers. These interactions served as great sources of information, motivation, support, and also reflected the value that parents placed on education. In fact, these invisible interactions served to provide much of the backbone for social mobility for rural families.

Notes

1 Most families purchased and raised one piglet so that they would have meat protein to eat during the year.
2 *Renminbi* is the currency in the People's Republic of China. At the time of the study, 1 U.S. dollar was equal to 8.29 *Yuan* (currency of the People's Republic of China).
3 Schools are often numbered: Number One primary school or Number Two middle school. They are not school quality rankings.

7 Migration for education

On one of my first visits to the education bureau that overseas Zhengxing, I stayed in a local hotel. The building was grey and stood nine stories high located directly across the street from one of the primary schools. At the time, the only way to enter my hotel room was to holler "*fuwuyuan*"[1] down the hall of each floor (one *fuwuyuan* was assigned to each floor). *Fuwuyuan* means service person and typically was a woman assigned to maintain the rooms on each floor. While I was visiting on this trip, the same *fuwuyuan*, Mrs. Li, was the attendant on my floor. Mrs. Li was curious that I was a single woman staying in a hotel that seemed to serve mostly male business clients. One morning while I was waiting for the elevator, I looked out the hotel window and watched as parents and children streamed into the primary school across the street. It was 7:45 a.m., and parents and children lined the streets surrounding the school gate, creating congestion on the road as cars, taxis, bicycles, and pedestrians stopped at the mouth of the school. I asked Mrs. Li if she was familiar with the primary school across the street. From the hotel window she pointed across the street to the Number Two primary school and told me that her son attended second grade at the school. She told me that she was not from this area, but was from a village in a more remote area and had moved to this area when her son started first grade so that her son could attend the local primary school. At the time, I wrote an entry about this situation in my notes, and although it was unique I did not imagine it would emerge as a strategy that rural parents engaged as part of their involvement in their children's schooling.

In the parental-involvement literature, moving school districts for the sake of a child's education is often characterized as an urban middle-class phenomenon because it takes planning and resources (Reay, 1998). A study in the United States by Swanson and Schneider (1999) found that mobility matters for students changing homes, but did result in a loss of social capital. In my study I found that rural families in Gansu also used migration as a parental-involvement strategy to support their children's education. High parental educational aspirations and seeking better quality learning environments fuel parents migrating for their children's schooling. All families that migrated in the study migrated because parents were dissatisfied with the educational quality in their home area.

The *hukou*[2] (户口) system, as discussed in Chapter 1, is a state tool for social control in China (Chan & Zhang, 1999). However, since the late 1970s, the restrictions on mobility have been loosened to allow for more mobility from rural areas to urban areas (Kwong, 2006). As part of China's economic development, millions of rural residents have migrated to urban centers in search of work. However, because of *hukou*, children of migrant workers wanting to attend schools face many challenges, including poor school quality and denied access to schooling (Koo, 2012; Kwong, 2011). Much of the research on the educational opportunities of migrant children in China has focused on migrant children in the cities or the children left behind in rural areas. The migration of rural families traveling between villages and townships is an area has been left largely unstudied, until this book.

To migrate from one area to another, families in my study drew on a combination of social networks and economic resources. Parents migrated for two reasons. First, it was a transition year in schooling and second to improve the overall schooling environment. Several families with whom I worked used their network of friends and families to gain entry for their children into the city schools. One way to gain entry into a city middle school is to sit for the city primary school exit examination. Two rural parents in my study used their connections to gain a seat for their sons to sit for the primary school examination in the local city. In order to enter the urban educational ladder of primary to middle school to high school, these families found a way to have their sons sit for the primary school examination, which would guarantee them a slot in the urban middle school. Both families believed that the curriculum and learning in the urban middle school would better prepare their children to enter high school. Moreover, high schools are only located in the cities, a structural feature of the educational system. Both rural families wanted to move their entire families to the cities. The other families that migrated in the study moved from more remote areas to the township level. All families carefully prepared for their migration, aligning resources, tapping into the support of friends and family, and even working through the bureaucracy to change their family or child's *hukou* status. The families presented in this chapter are not the only families to migrate in the study but exemplify the planned nature of such a move, along with the resources required to implement it.

Schooling transitions

Wu Shizhuang's family lived in the faculty dormitory at the preschool attached to the middle school. Mrs. Wu was a Chinese teacher at the middle school and the director of the preschool. Mr. and Mrs. Wu both farmed more than 10 *mu* of land. Mr. and Mrs. Wu both completed high school in the city, and Mrs. Wu received additional training in early childhood development in 2000, making her one of the most educated parents in my study. Wu Shizhuang had an older sister, Wu Rei, in eighth grade. Wu Rei attended the city middle school; she started her middle school career at the local middle school and transferred to the city middle school during the second semester of seventh grade.

During my visits to student homes, I often joined families during meal times. Parents would teach me how to cook and how to make handmade noodles. Most of my conversations in the Wu home occurred during meal times. While we were kneading the flour for noodles, Mrs. Wu told me that she wanted her children "to get out and understand and broaden their horizons. Schools can't do this, but as parents we can do this." Mr. and Mrs. Wu wanted their children to "walk out" of the village and sought out opportunities for their children. Mrs. Wu shared with me that her daughter, Wu Rei, was living in the city with her grandparents and attending the city middle school. Mrs. Wu explained to me why she had her daughter transfer to the city school:

> It might be that the middle school has better facilities, or another reason is that children will eventually study outside of here [rural areas] when they reach high school [all high schools are in urban areas].

Mrs. Wu describes both the superior facilities in the urban areas as well as her desire for social mobility for her children. She continued to say,

> It isn't that I think the school is better in the urban area it is that the scope of the school is larger than in our township, so they [students] have a broader view.

Mrs. Wu is a teacher in a rural school and is hesitant to make the explicit claim that the urban school is better. But, she does suggest that the urban school can expand the views of its students. The assumption she puts forth is that rural schools are limited. Mrs. Wu then suggested,

> But, I think there is a change, there are more and more people transferring from here to there. Their personalities are more open and they are freer in their speech and speak faster. I often tell [her] to slow down when she speaks, but I think I speak slowly. Actually, she used to speak slowly, and she really did not know how to talk. We want to move the whole family there [city]. . . . If our circumstances allow it and we have the opportunity to move to the city then we will move there.

Mrs. Wu sees the migration happening around her, the loosening of the *hukou* allowing residents with the means to move. Mrs. Wu echoes Mr. Lu's account in Chapter 2 about the openness of urban students compared with rural students. Mrs. Wu goes beyond the importance of education to "walk out" of the village to actually wanting the lifestyle of urban residents for her children. She believes that urban areas will expand the horizon for her children. After living in the urban area, her daughter speaks more quickly, and Mrs. Wu finds that her daughter now knows how to speak.

Mrs. Wu told me that Wu Rei had moved from the rural school to the urban school after Chinese New Year. I asked Mrs. Wu if it had been convenient to move to the city in the middle of the year. She told me:

> It is not too convenient because when my daughter transferred, we sought out Mr. Wang, who was a principal . . . my husband's cousin, not a close relative.

Having a relative in the school aided the transition for Wu Rei. Mr. Wu's mother accompanied Wu Rei to the city middle school. Grandmother Wu prepared meals for Wu Rei and made sure she attended school safely. Mrs. Wu explained to me that they waited to move:

> Also, we might be able to change our *hukou* (户口), household registry, we [Mr. and Mrs. Wu] both have rural *hukou* . . . before we move, our *hukou* will already be taken care of, but if we directly transfer, they might not accept us, therefore, he will take the primary school exit examination there . . . after the examinations he will go to that school [city middle]. . . . Both of them [the children] have urban *hukou*. If he [Wu Shizhuang] passes this upcoming examination [primary school exit examinations] he will automatically matriculate to a school [city middle school], then all his school fees and miscellaneous fees will be the same.

Mr. and Mrs. Wu both believed that the city schools would have better facilities and opportunities for their children to enter high school and beyond. They had been planning to migrate to the urban area for many years. The first step they took was to transfer their children's *hukou* to an urban *hukou* in 1996. Then, they used their kinship ties to transfer their daughter to the city middle school in 2003. Next, she told me, "Last year, we just moved our home to the city." They purchased a house in the city in preparation for the move to the city. Finally, they had their son sit for the primary school examination in the city so that he could automatically matriculate into the city middle school. All the steps that Mr. and Mrs. Wu took to migrate their family were invisible to the teachers in the rural areas. As a teacher, Mrs. Wu had the disposition to understand the educational field. She knew the difference between urban and rural curriculums and the importance of having her son sit for the primary exit examination in the city.

Mr. and Mrs. Wu were meticulous in preparing for the migration of the children and then themselves. Mr. Wu continued to farm the land in the rural areas. However, Mrs. Wu was transferred from the rural middle school to an elementary school in the urban area. Mr. and Mrs. Wu followed the legal protocols to migrate their family from having a rural *hukou* to an urban *hukou* in the same district. This migration from start to finish spanned a total of 12 years. This legal form of migration was not typical of other families in the study.

Migration to the cities

As we learned in the Chapters 2 and 5, the Hu family was interested in and very motivated to support their children's schooling, to the extent that they were willing to provide material resources for their children's schooling. During a visit to the Hu family, Mr. Hu explained to me that he felt that English teaching in the rural areas needed to be improved. When he was younger, learning English was optional, and teachers did not value and emphasize English language learning. In the context of talking about English-language learning, Mrs. Hu mentioned that she and Mrs. Wu had asked one of the middle school English teachers to tutor their sons in English. Both Mrs. Hu and Mrs. Wu wanted their sons to take the primary exit examination in the city and felt that the boys needed extra help with the English portion of the examination. Both families tapped into their economic resources to provide the extra tutoring need to prepare for the examination. Mrs. Hu used her social networks and asked one of her relatives in the city to obtain an extra copy of the primary school exit examination review papers. Mrs. Hu believed that the English lessons in the city provided a deeper understanding and she searched for a copy of the English textbook used in the city schools for the boys (Hu Zhuwan and Wu Shizhuang) to review. When I asked Mr. and Mrs. Hu why they wanted to have Hu Zhuwan sit for the examination in the city, they told me:

> His sister is going to test into high school in the city, I want to let him go there [city], and I will go cook for them. . . . There are no high schools in the rural areas, you have to go to the city.

When I asked Mrs. Hu if they would be migrating the whole family, she told me:

> Yes, it will be more convenient for the children . . . it is easier to have him take the test there [city]. To transfer later will be more troublesome. . . . I found someone to let them [Wu Shizhuang and Hu Zhuwan] sit for the examination there [in the city]. Usually, they do not allow it [rural students testing in urban areas as an urban student]. We expect to move in August.

The reasons Mr. and Mrs. Wu gave for wanting to have their son take the primary school examination were similar to the reasons that Mr. and Mrs. Hu gave: they expected that their sons would eventually enroll in high school and, as a result, it made practical sense to make the move now. Both of the families' daughters were or would be in the city schools, it made sense for the whole family to move together. Mr. and Mrs. Wu migrated in August by renting a small apartment on the outskirts of the city. Hu Zhuwan attended the urban middle school and tested into the Number Two High School in the urban area. It was interesting to note that migrating for school, or sending children to another area for schooling, was not unusual in this area. For the Hu family, the *hukou* situation was handled outside of changing their *hukou* registration.

Families did not just make rural to city migrations to improve academic outcomes for their children; they also moved among rural areas. Zhu Heqi's mother told me that her parents-in-law sent her brother-in-law to study in another province. She reported that the change in schools was good for him because he improved his grades and eventually completed high school. A few other rural parents with whom I worked had migrated their entire family to Junxi county where I conducted my research. These families were quite poor and had decided to migrate because their relatives told them the school environment was better in Zhengxing. These rural parents left their entire social networks, financial networks, and social supports behind in their home area to migrate to Zhengxing township. The Wang family did not formally migrate, but a grandparent moved with his grandchildren to Zhengxing in search of better schools. For the Gu and Qi families, they had relatives that had recently migrated to the county and that had encouraged both families to migrate. Both families were poor and lived more than six kilometers from Zhengxing primary school.

Wang Zhu's family lived in the mountains about 30 kilometers away from Zhengxing. She has an older sister in middle school, a younger sister also in sixth grade, and a younger brother in fourth grade. Wang Zhu's mother never attended school, and her father completed high school. Wang Zhu's grandfather brought all four children to Zhengxing to attend the primary and middle school. The Wang family rented a small shop on the main road next to restaurants, little shops, and a health clinic.

Wang Zhu's grandfather greeted me with a smile when I opened up the fluffy blanket curtain leading into their home. He was eager to have a visitor during the daytime, as he was lonely and did not have many things to do to pass the time. He lamented that except for having to prepare the meals, he had little to do. The home felt temporary, as there was a single old bed for the children and a small mat on the floor upon entering. The whole "home" was only 30 square feet. Grandfather Wu had a single bed in the hallway between the front of the room and the back of the room. At the back of the room was a small coal stove for cooking and to provide heat for the home. Grandfather Wang told me that he came alone with the children to Zhengxing because Wang Zhu's parents had to tend to the farm plots. Grandfather Wang was very happy to talk about his grandchildren. Similar to Grandmother Wu, Grandfather Wang was tasked with feeding the children and making sure they safely traveled to school. Grandfather Wang himself had only attended three years of schooling at the village school. Grandfather Wang often told me that schooling 50 years ago is very different from schools today. He said, "50 years ago, schooling was not like it is today, you only needed to recognize a few characters and little math." Grandfather Wang was diligent in keeping track of his grandchildren's grades and homework. He sat beside them as they studied, but was unable to review their homework. He would ask Wang Zhu's older sister Wang Le to review the homework. But, she did not return until between 8:45 p.m. to 9:00 p.m. in the evening, after the evening study hall. Wang Le also had to complete her own homework assignments in addition to reviewing her sibling's assignments.

When I asked Grandfather Wang why he accompanied the children, he quickly responded that he was not working and could cook a little. The farm work was too much for him now and left it to Wang Zhu's parents to care for the farm work. It was Wang Zhu's father's idea to relocate the children to Zhengxing, a township, instead of remaining in the village. Wang Zhu's older sister started middle school this year, so instead of spending money on paying for her to board in a dormitory, Mr. Wang decided to move all the children. With the shrinking village size, the village school had fewer children and was a multi-grade school. Grandfather Wang detailed the costs of such a move for the family, the cost of having to buy food, supplies for the children, and pay for the rental shop. Grandfather Wang emphasized that the costs were a heavy burden on the parents and that it was distracting for the children to be away from their parents. However, in his observation, the schooling in Zhengxing was more formal. In the village school, there was only one teacher for all the students. Seeking better schooling conditions for their children was a growing phenomenon in Zhengxing.

In search of better quality schools

The Gu family lived in the Xu Guang village, about six kilometers from the primary school, and were currently renting their home from a family member. Gu Baodu was 15 years old and had repeated second and fourth grade. Gu Baodu had one older brother who was 17 years old, Gu Jihua, and had completed middle school in their old county. Gu Jihua was not currently enrolled in school. During different visits to their home, Gu Jihua was either unemployed or engaged in temporary day labor. The Gu family did not own any land in Zhengxing. Mr. Gu currently worked in a mine and was usually away for three or more months at a time. Mrs. Gu had never attended school and Mr. Gu had only completed fifth grade.

Gu Baodu's family moved to Zhengxing county before the start of the school year. Mrs. Gu described to me her views on Gu Baodu's education:

> We just moved here from Juhua and the test scores there [Juhua schools] are terrible. He [Gu Baodu] just transferred here. . . . We just transferred here this year, I am adamant in my resolve that he [her son] has to go to school. I will support him financially to allow him to study.

I asked Mrs. Gu why they had decided to migrate to this area. She told me:

> The primary schools are better here . . . my relatives told me the schools here are better . . . all my relatives say that Zhengxing primary schools are better than our schools . . . all the examination scores are higher here [Zhengxing]. So, we decided to transfer our son here, to migrate here for his education. . . . The main goal of moving here was so that he [Gu Baodu] could go to school, and second to buy some land. But, mainly to provide him with the environment so that he could study.

When I asked Mrs. Gu to describe the schools in Juhua, she told me that

> it [Juhua] is small, there are few students. All the good teachers have been transferred elsewhere so all the teachers that are left are all incompetent. We are from a remote mountainous place. . . . My aunt is here, they migrated here earlier.

The way that Mrs. Gu evaluated the school quality in Juhua by assuming that the good teachers left and that the rural schools were left with incompetent teachers was similar to Mrs. Yao's (in Chapter 2) understanding of the poor educational conditions in rural areas.

110 *Migration for education*

The Gu family also used their kinship relationships to learn where better schools were in the area, even beyond their own county. They knew that it was difficult to get good teachers in a remote mountainous region and wanted to make sure that their youngest son would have the best schooling opportunities. So, mustering up all their resources for the move, they migrated to a new county, with the support of relatives. In the Western context, migrating for the purposes of a child's education was not typically seen as a behavior that poor families would take. For these poor families, migrating to a new area meant using most of their financial resources, leaving family and social networks, and living in an unfamiliar place for their children's education and future. However, all these efforts are still invisible to the teacher. Enrolling Gu Baodu for school in Zhengxing was visible to his teacher; however, the motivations behind the family migration were invisible. When I talked with Mrs. Gu[3], Gu Baodu's *banzhuren*, about Gu Baodu she did not know that his parents migrated to the area because of the better schools. She only knew that he was not from around here and was doing poorly in school. Gu Baodu ranked 224 out of 230 students in the district on the final sixth-grade district examination.

Qi Youkang's family: moving to a better place

Qi Youkang's family had migrated from Juhua county before the start of this school year. Mrs. Qi told me that the family had actually wanted to move several years ago:

> We have the *hukou* for this area now. We have only migrated here a little while. We wanted to bring the children here earlier; the schools are better here offering the children a better educational foundation. Now, I regret that I did not transfer the children here sooner.

But, the family's economic situation was not stable and a constant struggle. There was a death in the family in the preceding years that increased their expenses. Through Mrs. Qi's juxtaposition of the teaching quality of Zhengxing with her experiences in Juhua provided more evidence as to why she migrated the family for her son's education. She told me:

> They [the teachers in Zhengxing] are better at monitoring and teaching. . . . I've been [to the school in Juhua]. . . . The schools in Juhua are not like the schools here, others [Juhua teachers] do not monitor students. . . . Teachers teach the students and ask if they have such and such in their home. Then they [teachers] tell students to steal such and such from their dad, if there is an apricot or other fruit. They say, "you steal it for me" and instruct students to do such things. Goodness, sometimes this makes me so mad that I went to the school and gave the teacher a good talking to. . . . As a teacher, how can they say such things to children? . . . You support children to be thieves, to steal, you teach them these things. It makes me so mad that I scold them [teachers];

from preschool to first grade, they did not correctly give children the proper educational foundation.

Mrs. Qi was aware of the differences between the school quality in her old area, Juhua, and in Zhengxing. She blamed the teachers in Juhua for hindering her son's education because they did not properly teach him the basics. In Juhua, she was not afraid of going to school when she saw the school teaching things improperly. It is interesting to note, that Mrs. Qi may have made the same assumptions about rural schools as Mrs. Yao mentioned earlier, that teachers in rural areas may be there because they were not good teachers, otherwise they would have already moved onto to better schooling conditions. Mrs. Qi's anger about the teacher's behavior consumed her so much that it did not matter to whom she was talking.

Mrs. Qi observed and interacted with teachers on numerous occasions to improve her son's education and said, "This son [Qi Youkang] was born in Kaoying, and there the fundamentals were not well taught, teachers, I had a few encounters with teachers . . . that they did not teach the fundamentals well." "Teachers are not strict." When Mrs. Qi told me about her encounters with teachers in Kaoying her voice was confident and looked me directly in the eyes. But, lowered her eyes and the volume in her voice grew quieter as she explained to me that she did not dare to go to the schools in Zhengxing:

> I don't go, other people are literate, and I don't know anything. I won't know how to speak in front of the teacher. I don't know if what I say is right or wrong. Teachers have been good and caring. I am afraid to say the wrong thing. Gu Baodu's mother also is not educated, when we had been called in for a parent–teacher meeting she also did not dare go.

The bad teaching situation in Juhua provoked Mrs. Qi to move beyond her social position to scold a teacher. However, Mrs. Qi's account of her interaction with Zhengxing teachers, we can see her how her social position and disposition toward interacting with teachers influenced her willingness to interact with teachers. She was afraid that by being illiterate she might not say the right thing, which might impact her son's education.

Mr. and Mrs. Qi cared deeply about Qi Youkang's schooling, and they moved him to two different schools to improve his schooling opportunities. Qi Youkang started his schooling in their local primary school, preschool through second grade, but as mentioned above, Mrs. Qi found the schools and teachers to be of poor quality. Then, drawing on family support, they moved him in with his aunt during third through fifth grade. To have to separate from your child was a sacrifice, but one that Mrs. Qi was willing to make so that her son would have better schooling opportunities. Finally, they migrated to Zhengxing for his sixth grade. As mentioned earlier, Mrs. Qi had wanted to migrate the family sooner so that both her sons could take advantage of the schooling opportunities in the area. However, because they could not change their *hukou* earlier to this area, her older son's education had been compromised. She was sad and regretted that her older son had received a subpar education and was now working instead of being in middle school.

In her description of the differences between Juhua and Zhengxing, we can see that Mrs. Qi did not like the new area but was willing to sacrifice her own happiness for her son's schooling. She told me:

> Things are better there. . . . It is not as dry as it is here. . . . It is really windy here. . . . I am not use to it here. I don't love it at all, even now I don't it [here]. I am not accustomed to it here, even if I don't love it, there's nothing I can do, it is so dry here, I don't like the wind . . . I don't love it here.

Mr. and Mrs. Qi moved to Zhengxing for their children's education and because they had very little land in Juhua. Not only were the parents leaving an environment that was familiar, as demonstrated above, but also their social networks were no longer available to these families. In the previous chapter, families turned to their social networks for information and support and were most comfortable with them. Therefore, when families migrated, they not only sacrificed their own comfort with the new area but also their social networks for gathering information and support. Also, the Qi family had to live in a more remote area in Zhengxing because of their limited economic resources.

Both the Qis and the Gus used their invisible social networks to gather information about the academic environment in Zhengxing and migrated their families. However, the motivation for this major life change, migrating, was invisible to Gu Baodu and Qi Youkang's teachers. Mrs. Gu, their homeroom teacher, knew that both students were new to the area and told me that these parents did not care about their sons' schooling because neither parents visited the school. Mrs. Gu told me that she invited (passed on the message via Gu Baodu and Qi Youkang)

> the parents [Mr. and Mrs. Qi] several times, but they never came to the school. The student does not studiously complete his homework. Usually, I have many activities, meetings and such and such . . . so there are some things I forget to do [seek out the students who need help]. I expect that the students will come to me when they need help. I want to teach them. . . . From their tests you can see that he does not know many characters, in class he has extreme difficulty when he reads a section aloud in class.

I observed both Gu Baodu and Qi Youkang mumble the class reading and when Mrs. Gu calls for volunteers in class they both stare at their desks as if the answer will appear in the chipped spots of the desk. Gu Baodu and Qi Youkang were poor-performing students, and Mrs. Gu wanted to meet with their parents, but neither the Gus nor the Qis met with Mrs. Gu. It was possible that Gu Baodu and Qi Youkang did not tell their parents that their presence was requested in the school. The most common form of communication between teachers and parents was via the student. By not giving information to their parents, Gu Baodu and Qi Youkang took responsibility for their own learning but also served to limit the support their parents gave them. We can see that the physical visible presence of parents was important to the teacher, Mrs. Gu.

Conclusion

In this chapter I have described how rural parents moved their families at critical schooling transition points and in search of better educational opportunities. Migrating a family for schooling clearly shows that rural parents are not passive, backward, or in anyway lacking in ability. They are actively engaged and involved in supporting their children's schooling. Moreover, this strategy is sophisticated and akin to the strategies used by urban Chinese parents as well as middle-class Western families.

As discussed in previous chapters, rural parents were critically aware of their social position and how their limited academic abilities shaped their disposition toward supporting their children's schooling. Rural parents emphasized that children needed to take responsibility for their own school learning because parents themselves had limited academic aptitude. In fact, I found that most rural parents held high educational aspirations, emphasized their child's own agency in terms of academic learning, and implemented strategies to support their children's schooling. The specific strategies that rural parents engaged included migrating their families to provide a better schooling experience. Through rural parents' own existing networks they gathered educational information, including test scores and general knowledge, about the teachers and schools. Rural families migrated to areas with better schools, including moving within and between counties. The carefully planning, collecting, and connecting economic and social resources to migrate a family in search of better schooling conditions speaks volumes about rural parent's invisible involvement in their children's schooling.

Rural parents working to help their children move up the social ladder willingly left behind their homes in search of better educational opportunities. As China continues to develop and society grows more stratified, parents will search for better learning environments for their children. Rural parents are savvy about the *hukou* system and understand when and how to work within or around it to gain access to better schooling conditions for their children. For the Wu and Hu families, the move went smoothly and drew deeply on their social and economic networks. For the Wang, Qi, and Gu families, the results of the migration are unclear. These families had fewer economic and social resources and moved from more remote areas where the quality of schooling was not as strong as Zhengxing. Moreover, teachers are unfamiliar with the new families, the dialect barrier, and overall economic conditions of the families. All families should be applauded for migrating, however, this invisible form of parental involvement is invisible by teachers in the schools. In the case of Gu Baodu and Qi Youkang, their poor schooling was only compounded when they attended a better school and the boys fell even further behind. As remarkable as this strategy is for rural parents, it also poses a potential threat to equity in rural areas. The resources in rural areas are slowly also migrating toward urban centers, leaving fewer and fewer school resources in rural areas, which are already lacking resources.

Notes

1 Literally translated as wait staff. A generic term used for individuals working in the service industry, including hotels and restaurants.
2 The household registry is a hereditary residency permit system that divides residents according to their occupation and place of residence into broad categories of urban and rural. Allocation of grain rations, availability of housing, health care, education, and employment are based on one's household residency. For example, a rural resident with a rural *hukou* is not able to gain employment, education, or health care in the city. In recent years, the government has loosened some of the constraints of the *hukou* system.
3 Mrs. Gu (teacher) is not related to Gu Baodu.

Conclusion

This book reveals that rural parents engage in invisible forms of parental involvement in their children's schooling through active strategic planning, gathering information, and providing positive learning environments for their children. They disrupt the image and discourse of rural peasants being lazy and backward; rural parents in this study demonstrate their strategy of parental involvement in their children's schooling. Rural parents describe the hardships of living in rural areas, barriers that they face educating their children in schools and communities that are underresourced, and the challenges and opportunities of China's modernization. This more nuanced understanding of rural parents demonstrates that they are not lazy or uncaring but in fact, when faced with new interactions in schools and in the home, parents are thoughtful, realistic, and savvy as to how they are involved in their children's schooling. In order for their children to "walk out" of the village, all the rural parents in this study were actively involved in their children's schooling. Central to their strategy is holding high educational aspirations and placing the responsibility for learning responsibility on the student themselves, then parents prepare resources for their children, gather academic information to support their children, and provide a good learning environment for their children. Rural parents engage their parental involvement strategies dynamically. Unfortunately, much of their involvement is missed in the current discussion as rural parents are often dismissed as being backward, lacking, and not involved in their children's schooling.

Framing

The language used by rural parents to describe their involvement in their children's schooling mirrors China's pursuit of cultivating modern and quality citizens. Rural parents describe resources in rural areas as lacking and in need of improvement, echoing China's development discourse that rural areas and people need to be improved. However, from the perspective of rural parents, we learn that although the previous generation in this area did not value education, this generation of parents in my study now emphatically speaks about the importance of education for their children's future. Rural parents in the study explain that the previous generation (their parents) did not value education and often withdrew children from schooling to help the family. In this area, rural parents report a shift in the value of education; they themselves now value education for their children after experiencing and seeing economic and social changes in China – families in the study now direct family resources toward supporting their children's education. Through parental experiences of having little education and wealth and being shaped in a context where parents did not value education to now living in a society that highly values education, we understand why rural parents disposition towards schooling, now placing a value on education as a pathway for their children's future. It is important to note that previous studies often ascribe certain characteristics to poor rural families, but this is one of the first studies that specifically focuses on the lives of poor rural parents. Rural parents did not want their children living the same harsh lives that they lived, and they viewed education as a requirement their children needed in order to become dragons and phoenixes and "walk out" of the village.

The concept of *suzhi* is commonly expressed in education in terms of improving the quality of an individual to support the functioning of the nation. The two concepts of *suzhi* and cultural capital are similar in that they seek to explain how power, status, and privilege are acquired. *Suzhi* assumes that one's intelligence and ability results in achieving power, status, and privilege whereas cultural capital points more to structural, economic, and social interactions that privilege one class over another. There is a clear connection between *suzhi* and cultural capital in terms of describing social stratification, desire for social mobility, and room for rural parents to assist in social mobility. In this study, although parents have limited experience with schools, parents are not idle but are actively working toward supporting their children's schooling. The conceptual model and strategy parents engage demonstrates that rural parents have high *suzhi* to mobilize resources, but currently their work goes unnoticed both in the parental involvement literature as well as in the Chinese context.

Agency

Drawing upon and expanding Bourdieu's concept of habitus, field, and capital, we see how rural parental involvement is dynamic and rural parental habitus is shaped and reshaped. Mrs. Qi shows that in one context in her home county she was willing to confront the teacher, but in the new county, Zhengxing, Mrs. Qi is unwilling to meet with the teachers. In her home county, Mrs. Qi is dismayed by the wrongdoing of the teacher and angry about how the teacher's actions will impact her children. However, in Zhengxing, Mrs. Qi believes the quality of schools is better and is afraid to go to the schools. It is noteworthy that rural parents shared many of the behaviors of urban Chinese parents (Fong, 2004) and middle-class families in the U.S. and England (Reay, 1998; Lareau, 2000). Comparing rural behaviors with urban parents does not imply that the urban or Western way is the correct form of parental involvement. In fact, this study offers more insight into the invisible forms of parental involvement that rural parents engage to support their children's schooling.

Conclusion 117

Rural parents do not allow their economic and social positions to determine their future and actively work toward improving the academic future for their children. All rural families worked tirelessly to create positive learning environments for their children. Within China's economic and social reforms, *hukou* changes have loosened up the physical space for rural residents allowing for rural mobility. In order to cultivate educational opportunities for their children, their actions alter and challenge assumptions of rural parent apathy and backwardness. By studying the dispositions of rural parents as they engage with schools, community, and in the home with their children, we learn how parental dispositions are reshaped as parents engage strategies to support their children's schooling. Moreover, we learn how rural parents shape the dispositions of their children as they emphasize that academic learning is the responsibility of the student.

Rural parents tapped into preexisting networks to gather academic information, academic help, and educational opportunities and worked hard to provide resources to improve the learning environment of their children. Rural parents work hard, physically, mentally, and emotionally to provide a good learning environment for their children. What is remarkable is that parent work is not limited by educational level or wealth. Although the range of wealth levels was quite compact, I did notice that across all ranges, rural parents worked multiple jobs to support their children's education. Similar to Chinese parents in Fong's study in urban Dalian, rural parents in this study supported their children's education through making sacrifices of time and money. Rural parents were more than willing to take on additional paid work to pay for school tuition, other expenses, and provide supplementary educational materials for their children. In contrast to rural families in Lin's study (1993), rural parents in this study provided their children with dedicated time to complete their homework; rural parents actively relieved their children of household chores during the week so that their children could focus their efforts on studying. The sacrifice of relieving their children of chores combined with the additional workload that parents took on had a physical and emotional impact on rural parents. Rural parents' descriptions of how important education was to their children's future echoed China's modernization proclamations over the last 20 years. This component of parental involvement further demonstrates the *suzhi* that rural parents embody, as most parents grew up in a time when education was not considered important. Rural parents hold high educational aspirations, as mentioned above, and as such understand the importance of studying and completing assignments; therefore, rural parents create dedicated studying time for their children.

The practice of families migrating to provide a better schooling environment for their children as an invisible form of parental involvement is incredible. Given the Chinese context that limits physical mobility and in effect social mobility, for rural families to gather the information, prepare the resources, and actually migrate to a strange place for their child's education is no small feat. Simply ascribing backward and lacking traits to rural parents and not actually investigating the behaviors of rural parents we miss the active and creative involvement of rural parents. Moreover, limiting this study to only rural parents and not in comparison to urban parents in China not only prevents a deficit model of rural parental involvement but also creates space to fully understand rural parental involvement in their children's schooling. When you consider that the rural families in my study have few resources and limited education in terms of literacy, it is even more exciting to learn the pathways they maneuver to support their children's schooling. The two families that migrated during a critical transition time to the urban area had slightly higher education levels and economic resources. However, all families spent considerable time planning and preparing for their migration.

Within the Chinese migration literature, the focus has been on migration for work and the subsequent impact on children of migrant workers, including left-behind children. Findings in this book on migrating families for education offer an exciting contribution to the migration literature. Migration for education creates new challenges for schools in terms of having students unfamiliar with the local dialect, having received different curriculum, and also the adjustment for children and their families into new environments. The examples of the Qi and Gu family migrating from another county illustrate the challenges faced by families migrating for education. First, teachers are unaware of the children's previous learning, have some difficulty with the dialect, and have difficulty communicating with parents. A major concern with migration for education is the loss of social capital (Swanson & Schneider, 1999). The Gu and Qi family do not own any land in Zhengxing and are pushed to living in the farthest outskirts of the district. They do not have family and friends, and are physically so far removed that it is difficult to create new social networks.

Implications

This book offers the mechanism for understanding how rural parents are involved in their children's schooling. These strategies are important for the educational policy community to understand, evaluate, and possibly cultivate. Current parental-involvement policies in China have placed an emphasis on visible forms of parental involvement, such as talking to teachers, visiting schools, and participating in parent–teacher meetings. In contrast, the poor rural families with whom I worked engaged in invisible sacrifices and strategies to support their children's schooling. These invisible forms of involvement are similar to those used by urban Chinese parents (Fong, 2004; Lin, 1993). There was a concerted effort on the part of rural parents to support their children's education. Rural parents had a critical understanding and awareness of their social position and how their limited education and wealth shaped their knowledge and ability to support their children's education. However, this did not necessarily translate into having little educational information. On the contrary, rural parents engaged in strategies that leveraged their resources to make schooling a hospitable experience for their children. Rural parents first and foremost held high educational aspirations and believed that their children were responsible for their own academic learning. In conjunction with holding high educational aspirations and placing the responsibility for academic learning on the students, parents purposefully gathered academic information, provided schooling materials, and migrated their families to better schools.

Connecting parents in the school

Rural parents with whom I worked were active and interested in their children's schooling and were not indifferent, as they are often portrayed. Most rural parents participated in invisible forms of parental involvement. Visible forms of parent–teacher relationships are currently being suggested by policy initiatives. However, given that they lack understanding and experience with schools, rural parents will need support in participating in visible forms of parental involvement. At the same time, I believe that teachers and administrators need to become more cognizant of the invisible forms of involvement that rural parents engaged in to support their children's schooling. This is important for two reasons. First, teachers and administrators could help rural parents realize that what they have done is, indeed, quite valuable in their children's schooling. Second, it may help teachers be more conscious of their own biases of rural parents. Mrs. Gu came to the realization that she should talk to parents. During our meetings and discussions she would tell me that she was a rural resident and knew what it was like to be a rural parent. Towards the end of my study in one of our last meetings, Mrs. Gu reflected and told me that she realized she should and needed to talk to parents.

Having rural parents participate in some visible forms of involvement will not only be important to teachers but will also provide parents with knowledge about what their children are doing, and what they are supposed to be doing. Parents should not be tearing up their children's textbooks, like Mrs. Yao, and more visible involvement will enable parents to gain information and gain back some of their authority as parents.

Working-class parents in the American and English contexts have been described as being less effective than middle-class parents in their interactions with teachers (Lareau 2000; Reay, 1998). Based on their own educational experiences and social position, working-class parents have fewer tools to help them understand and work with teachers to benefit their children's schooling. Similarly, rural parents in this study expressed concern over their ability to talk directly with teachers. Several parents were afraid they would say the wrong thing and that this would negatively impact their children's schooling. Moreover, rural parents described teachers as the educational expert, and only in extreme situations would parents question the actions of the teachers.

Although not all the strategies that rural parents engaged in were successful, rural parents did actively support their children's education. In fact, some of the strategies that rural parents employed were sophisticated and akin to those of urban Chinese parents. When parents interacted in their social networks, they may not have been gaining the most accurate information. For example, when

Chang Bao and Wen Yijin's fathers talked with their child's principal, who was their old school mate, they were not gaining valid information about how their children were performing in school. In their social visit with their friend, Mr. Wen and Mr. Chang gained information about school and academic issues in general, I believe that school could take advantage of the social networks between these fathers and the principal. Rural parents mentioned that they attended school events, parent-teacher meetings, visited the school, and interacted with their friends. Local schools could develop parent-teacher workshops run by the principal to connect parents with teachers.

To aid rural parents building in their relationships with the school, a parent–teacher liaison could serve as a go-between for the parents and teachers. As a researcher, parents were comfortable talking to me about their concerns in their children's schooling. Rural parents with whom I worked knew that I had an understanding of their children's school life and spent time in the school talking with the teachers. Even though they understood that I was not affiliated with the school, rural parents often asked me to relay their concern and support for their children's schooling to the teachers. A parent–school liaison could be positioned as being affiliated with the school and having knowledge of the dominant culture but also knowledgeable about the habitus of rural parents. Moreover, this person would not have any influence over children's grades so that parents could speak freely about their concerns. But, the liaison could convey parental support and concern to teachers for parents. The liaison could also help forge parent–teacher relationships to help parents feel more comfortable in the school, be more visible, and to help teachers understand parental concerns.

Rural teachers expressed their concern that the poor-performing parents in my study did not care about their children's schooling because they ignored numerous teacher requests to come to the school. Rural parents raised the same concern that they did not know when to visit the schools. The practice of having the student convey the teacher's message was problematic because children who were poor-performing may feel ashamed and not want to be scolded by their parents or the teacher. Mr. Wu suggested that teachers should tell the student's friends or a neighborhood child to relay messages from the teacher, because he found out that his son was not relaying messages to him. This was important in rural areas because verbal instructions are the main form of communication between parents and schools, especially because many parents were illiterate or had low literacy skills. A parent liaison, or having a neighborhood child convey teacher messages, would aid in the communication between parents and teachers so that teachers do not misinterpret parental non-attendance in schools as uncaring of their children's education. Mrs. Gu's own reflection and suggestions that although she herself is a rural parent, she may not fully understand rural parents perspectives and could reach out to her students and families. These findings will help administrators and teachers in rural contexts better understand how to connect with parents to improve the educational conditions for children.

Future directions

The new focus in China on parental involvement in a child's education and the proposed expansion of parent education schools might well create new expectations for parental involvement. However, the current attitudes of rural parents have not been flattering. I encourage policymakers and planners to understand the reasons why parents may be hesitant to come directly into schools and to work within the comfort zone of parents. During my fieldwork, I visited a few parent–teacher meetings in one city middle school and in one high school, and found that parents were seated in student desks and listened as teachers lectured them on ways they could be more helpful to the school, including ensuring that their children arrived earlier to class, purchased vitamins to improve mental capacity, and purchase materials to improve English language skills. Teachers prescribed parental support, and there was little effort to encourage a co-creation of parent–teacher support. Some researchers have suggested that schools dictate or prescribe the role of parents in terms of their involvement in schools (Smrekar & Cohen-Vogel, 2001). To some extent, this may be productive in Gansu; currently, the school is not reaching out to parents and defining a role for them at all. As my book has demonstrated, rural parents were interested and active in their children's schooling; however, many rural parents' efforts were invisible to teachers and schools. Family-education schools are a good vehicle for conveying the role schools expect parents to play in supporting their children's schooling as well as the expectations parents have of teachers. Rural parents expect that teachers manage their children and provide them with the skills to be successful in schools.

This book has focused on rural parents of children in sixth grade. This was an appropriate age-group for my research, but it does limit any discussion of parental involvement of older children in rural China. Sixth grade is the final grade of primary school, and children usually matriculate from there into middle school, but this is also the first transition in schooling where dropout begins. Compulsory education in China provides for free education for children in grades one through nine. Rural children in my study were usually free of the stress and competitiveness of examination pressures. Primary school is also typically where the most parental involvement occurs. The transition from middle school to high school naturally coincides with a steep decline in students as competitiveness and filtering reduces the student pool. Rural parents of students who succeed past this point usually have high-performing children. Therefore, future studies that investigate how parental involvement changes over these transitions will shed additional light on the relationship between parental involvement and student outcomes.[1]

Poverty and poor schooling conditions continue to exist in rural areas and shape the schooling environments for children and families. But, despite lacking in resources, rural parents in this study are not passive, have strong parent efficacy, and do focus their resources in ways that support their children's schooling. A new direction in the policy discussion could be to shift away from referencing rural areas as being backward and lacking to looking for ways that rural residents are active and engaged. Perhaps future work can explore more the active behaviors of rural parents to support their children's schooling and connect the behaviors to schooling outcomes. Evaluating schooling outcomes are beyond the scope of the current book. Poor schooling was identified as the main reason for families migrating for education. A more in-depth look at factors and patterns of migration for education would be very helpful for policymakers as well as for teachers and administrators. Like the "Old Man Moves a Mountain," slowly and with each generation, rural parents are moving forward and up the social ladder.

Note

1 See Kim and Fong (2013) for urban China.

Bibliography

Bourdieu, P. (1977a). Cultural reproduction and social reproduction. In J. Karabel and A.H. Halsey, *Power and ideology in education.* New York: Oxford University Press.
Bourdieu, P. (1977b). *Outline of a theory of practice.* Cambridge: Cambridge University Press.
Bourdieu, P. (1984). *Distinction.* London: Routledge.
Bourdieu, P. (1985). Social space and the genesis of groups. *Theory and Society,* 14(6): 723–744.
Bourdieu, P. (1990). *In other words: essays towards a reflexive sociology.* Cambridge: Polity Press.
Bourdieu, P. (1991). *Language and symbolic power.* Cambridge: Harvard University Press.
Bourdieu, P. & Wacquant, L. (1992). *An invitation to reflexive sociology.* Chicago: University of Chicago Press.
Brown, P. (2002). Parental investment in children's human capital in rural china. *China Education Forum,* 3(1): 6–10.
Buchmann, C. (2002). Getting ahead in Kenya: social capital, shadow education, and achievement. In B. Fuller and E. Hannum (Ed.), *Schooling and social capital in diverse cultures.* London: Elsevier Science.
Bu Xi. (2004). *Education bureau report.* Bu Xi: Bu Xi City.
Carbonaro, W.J. (1998). A little help from my friend's parents: intergenerational closure and educational outcomes. *Sociology of Education,* 71(4): 295–313.
Carolan-Silva, A. (2011). Negotiating the roles of community member and parent: participation in education in rural Paraguay. *Comparative Education Review,* 55(2): 252–270.
Chan, A., Madsen, R., & Unger, J. (1992). *Chen Village under Mao and Deng.* Berkeley: University of California Press.
Chan, K. & Zhang, L. (1999). The *hukou* system and rural-urban migration: processes and changes. *The China Quarterly,* 160(1): 818–855.
Chao, R. (1996). Chinese and European American mothers beliefs about the role of parenting in children's school success. *Journal of Cross-Cultural Psychology,* 27(4): 403–423.
Chao, R. (2000). The parenting of immigrant Chinese and European American mothers: relations between parenting styles, socialization goals, and parental practices. *Journal of Applied Developmental Psychology,* 21(2): 233–248.
Cheng, K.-M. (1996). *The quality of primary education: a case study of Zhejiang Province, China.* Paris: Institute for International Planning.

Bibliography

Chi, J. & Rao, N. (2003). Parental beliefs about school learning and children's educational attainment: evidence from rural China. *Ethos*, 31(3): 330–356.

Cohen, M. (1993). Cultural and political inventions in modern China: The case of the Chinese "Peasant." *Daedalus*, 122: 151–170.

Coleman, J. S. (1988). Social capital in the creation of human capital. *American Journal of Sociology*, 94: 95–120.

Connelly, R. & Zheng, Z. (2003). Determinants of primary and middle school enrollment of 10–18 year olds in China. *Economics of Education Review*, 22(4): 379–388.

Davis, D. (1989). Chinese social welfare: policies and outcomes. *The China Quarterly*, 119: 577–597.

Dauber, S. L., Alexander, K. L., & Entwisle, D. R. (1996). Tracking and transitions through middle grades: channeling educational trajectories. *Sociology of Education*, 69(4): 290–307.

Dello-Iacova, B. (2009). Curriculum reform and 'quality education' in China: an overview. *International Journal of Educational Development*, 29: 241–249.

Desimone, L. (1999). Linking parent involvement with student achievement: do race and income matter? *The Journal of Educational Research*, 93(1): 11–30.

Diamond, J. B., Ling, W., & Gomez, K. (2004). African American parents' educational orientations: the importance of social class and parent perceptions of schools. *Education and Urban Society*, 36(4): 383–427.

Dumais, S. A. (2002). Cultural capital, gender, and school success: the role of habitus. *Sociology of Education*, 75(1): 44–68.

Dumais, S. A. (2006). Early childhood cultural capital, parental habitus, and teachers' perceptions. *Poetics*, 34: 83–107.

Education Law of the People's Republic of China. In Chapter VI, Education and the society, Article 49, http://www.moe.edu.cn/english/laws_e.htm, accessed 3/3/08.

Entwisle, D. R., Alexander, J. L., & Olson, L. S. (2005). First grade and educational attainment by age 22: a new story. *American Journal of Sociology*, 110(5): 1458–1502.

Epstein, J. (1987). Toward a theory of family-school connections: teacher practices and family involvement. In K. Kurrelmann, F. Kaufman, & F. Lasel (Eds.). *Social intervention: potential and constraints*. New York: De Gruyter.

Epstein, J. (2001). *School, family, and community partnerships: preparing educators and improving schools*. Boulder: Westview Press.

Fan, C. (2008). Migration, hukou, and the Chinese city. In S. Yusuf & A. Saich, *China urbanizes: consequences, strategies, and policies* (pp. 65–90). Washington, DC: The World Bank.

Fan, X. (2001). Parental Involvement and students' academic achievement: a growth modeling analysis. *The Journal of Experimental Education*, 70(1), 27–61.

Fei, X. (1939). *Peasant life in China: a field study of country life in the Yangtze Valley*. New York: Dutton.

Fong, V. (2004). *Only hope: coming of age under China's one-child policy*. Stanford: Stanford University Press.

Gomes, M. (1984). Family size and educational attainment in Kenya. *Population and Development Review*, 10, 647–660.

Goyette, K. & Conchas, G. (2001). Family and non-family roots of social capital among Vietnamese and Mexican American children. In B. Fuller & E. Hannum (Eds.), *Schooling and social capital in diverse cultures*. London: Elsevier Science.

Greenhalgh, S. (2010). *Cultivating global citizens: population in the rise of China*. Cambridge, MA: Harvard University Press.

Greenhalgh, S. & Winckler, E. (2005).*Governing China's population: from Leninist to neoliberal biopolitics*. Palo Alto: Stanford University Press.

Gu, W. (2008). New horizons and challenges in China's public schools for parental involvement. *Education*, 128(4): 570–578.

Hannum, E. (1999). Political change and the urban-rural gap in basic education in China 1949–1990. *Comparative Education Review*, 43(2), 193–211.

Hannum, E. (2003). Poverty and Basic Education in Rural China: villages, households, and girls' and boys' enrollment. *Comparative Education Review*, 47(2).

Hannum, E., Kong, P., & Zhang, Y. (2009). Family sources of educational gender inequality in rural China: a critical assessment. *International Journal of Educational Development*, 29: 474–486.

Hannum, E. & Park, A. (2002). Educating China's rural children in the 21st century. *Harvard China Review*, 3(2), 8–14.

Hanson, M. & Pang, C. (2010). Idealizing individual choice: work, love, and family in the eyes of young, rural Chinese. In M. Halskov Hansen and R. Svarerud (Eds.), *iChina: The rise of the individual in modern Chinese society* (pp. 39–64). Copenhagen: NIAS-Nordic Institute of Asian Studies.

Hao, L., Hu, A., & Lo, J. (2014). Two aspects of the rural-urban divide and educational stratification in China: a trajectory analysis. *Comparative Education Review*, 58(3): 509–536.

Hill, N. E. & Taylor, L. C. (2004). Parental school involvement and children's academic achievement: pragmatic and issues. *Current Directions in Psychological Science*, 13(4): 161–164.

Ho, E. & Willms, J. (1996). Effects on parental involvement on eighth-grade achievement. *Sociology of Education*, 69(2): 126–141.

Hoover-Dempsey, K. V., Battiato, A. C., Walker, J.M.T., Reed, R. P., DeJong, J. M., & Jones, K. P. (2001). Parental involvement in homework. *Educational Psychologist*, 36(3): 195–209.

Horvat, E. M., Weinenger, E. B., & Lareau, A. (2003). From social ties to social capital: class differences in the relations between schools and parent networks. *American Educational Research Journal*, 40(2): 319–351.

Jacka, T., Kipnis, A., & Sargeson, S. (2013). *Contemporary China: society and social change*. Cambridge: Cambridge University Press.

Jaeger, M. (2011). Does cultural capital really affect academic achievement? new evidence from combined sibling and panel data. *Sociology of Education*, 84(4): 281–298.

Lawrence-Lightfoot, S. (2004). *The essential conversation: what parents and teachers can learn from each other.* New York: Random House.

Kalmijn, M. & Kraaykamp, G. (1996). Race, cultural capital, and schooling: an analysis of trends in the United States. *Sociology of Education*, 69(1): 22–34.

Kelliher, D. (1994). Chinese communist political theory and the rediscovery of the peasantry. *Modern China*, 20, 387–411.

Kim, S. & Fong, V. (2013). How parents help children with homework in China: narratives across the life span. *Asia Pacific Education Review*, 14: 581–592.

Kipnis, A. (1997). *Producing Guanxi: sentiment, self, and subculture in a north China village*. Durham: Duke University Press.

Kipnis, A. (2001). The disturbing educational discipline of "peasants. *The China Journal*, 46: 1–24.

Kipnis, A. (2011a). *Governing educational desire: culture, politics, and schooling in China*. Chicago, IL: University of Chicago Press.

Kipnis, A. (2011b). Subjectification and education for quality in China. *Economy and Society*, 40(2): 289–306.
Kong, P. (2003). *She'll belong to another family anyway: education, wealth and gender in rural China*. Unpublished Qualifying Paper, Harvard Graduate School of Education, Cambridge.
Kong, P. (2010). "To walk out": rural parents' views on education. *China: An International Journal*, 8(2): 360–373.
Koo, A. (2012). Is there any chance to get ahead? Education aspirations and expectations of migrant families in China. *British Journal of Sociology of Education*, 33: 547–564.
Kwong, J. 2006. The integration of migrant children in Beijing schools. In G. Postiglione (Ed.), *Education and social change in China: inequality in a market economy*. Armonk, New York: M. E. Sharpe.
Kwong, J. (2011). Education and identity: the marginalisation of migrant youths in Beijing. *Journal of Youth Studies*, 14: 871–883.
Lareau, A. (1987). Social class differences in family-school relationships: the importance of cultural capital. *Sociology of Education*, 60: 73–85.
Lareau, A. (1987, 2000). *Home advantage*. Lanham: Rowman and Littlefield.
Lareau, A. (2003). *Unequal childhoods: class, race, and family life*. Berkeley: University of California Press.
Lawrence-Lightfoot, S. (2004). *The essential conversation*. New York: Ballantine Books.
Lee, J.-S. & Bowen, N. (2006). Parental involvement, cultural capital, and the achievement gap among elementary school children. *American Educational Research Journal*, 43(2): 193–218.
Lewin, K., Little, A., Xu, H., & Zhen, J. (1994). *Educational innovation in China: Tracing the impact of the 1985 reforms*. Harlow, Essex: Longman.
Lewin, K. W. & Yingjie. (1994). *Implementing basic education in China: progress and prospects in rich, poor and national minority areas*. Paris: International Institute for Educational Planning.
Lin, J. (1993). *Education in post-Mao China*. Westport: Praeger.
Ma, X. & Guo, B. (1995). *An evaluation of parent schools in China: action research in family and early childhood*. Paris: United Nations Educational, Scientific, and Cultural Organization.
Mapp, K. (2003). Having their say: parents describe why and how they are engaged in their children's learning. *The School Community Journal*, 13(1): 35–64.
Maxwell, J.A. (1996). *Qualitative research design: an interactive approach* (Vol. 41). Thousand Oaks: Sage.
MacLeod, J. (1987). *Ain't no makin' it: leveled aspirations in a low-income neighborhood*. Boulder: Westview Press.
McNeal, R.B.J. (1999). Parental involvement as social capital: differential effectiveness on science achievement, truancy, and dropping out. *Social Forces*, 78(1): 117–144.
Miles, M.B. & Huberman, A. M. (1994). *An expanded sourcebook: qualitative data analysis*. Thousand Oaks: Sage.
Murphy, R. (2004a). Turning peasants into modern Chinese citizens: "population quality" discourse, demographic transition and primary education. *The China Quarterly*, 177: 1–20.
Murphy, R. (2004b). *How migrant labor is changing rural China*. Cambridge, UK: Cambridge University Press.
Naftali, O. (2009). Empowering the child: children's rights, citizenship, and the state in contemporary China. *The China Journal*, 61: 79–103.

Parcel, T. & Dufur, M. (2001). Capital at home and at school: effects on student achievement. *Social Forces*, 79: 881–912.
Parcel, T., Dufur, M. & Zito, R. (2010). Capital at home and at school: a review and synthesis. *Journal of Family and Marriage*, 72: 828–846.
Patton, M. Q. (1990). *Qualitative evaluation and research methods.* Thousand Oaks, CA: Sage.
Pena, D. C. (2001). Parental involvement: influencing factors and implications. *The Journal of Educational Research*, 94(1): 42–54.
Pomeranz, E., Moorman, E., & Litwack, S. (2007). The how, whom, and why of parents' involvement in children's academic lives: more is not always better. *Review of Educational Research*, 77(3): 373–410.
Pong, S-L. (1997). Sibship and educational attainment in peninsular Malaysia: do policies matter. *Sociological Perspectives*, 40(2), 227–242.
Qiao, F., Rozelle, S. , Huang, J., Zhang, L., & Luo, R. (2014). Road expansion and off-farm work in rural China. *The China Quarterly*, 218: 428–451.
Reay, D. (1998). *Class work: understanding mother's involvement in their children's primary schooling.* London: London University Press.
Reay, D. (2000). A useful extension of Bourdieu's conceptual framework?: emotional capital as a way of understanding mothers' involvement in their children's education? *The Sociological Review*, 48: 568–585.
Reay, D. (2004). 'It's all becoming habitus': beyond the habitual use of habits in educational research. *British Journal of Sociology of Education*, 25(4): 431–444.
Rose, P. (2003). Community participation in school policy and practice in Malawi. *Compare*, 33(1): 47–64.
Sayer, A. (2005). *The moral significance of class.* Cambridge: Cambridge University Press.
Schneider, B. & Coleman, J. S. (Eds.). (1993). *Parents, their children, and schools.* Boulder: Westview Press.
Sewell, W. & Shah, V. (1968). Parents' education and children's educational aspirations and achievements. *American Sociological Review*, 33(2): 191–209.
Smrekar, C. & Cohen-Vogel, C. (2001). The voices of parents: rethinking the intersection of family and school. *Peabody Journal of Education*, 76(2): 75–100.
Stevenson, H. W., Lee, S.-Y., & Stigler, J. W. (1986). Mathematics achievement of children in China and the United States. *Child Development*, 61: 1053–1067.
Stevenson, H. W. & Stigler, J. W. (1992). *The learning gap : why our schools are failing and what we can learn from Japanese and Chinese education.* New York: Summit Books.
Suzuki, I. (2002). Parental participation and accountability in primary schools in Uganda. *Compare*, 32(2): 243–259.
Swanson, C. & Schneider, B. (1999). Students on the move: residential and educational mobility in American's schools. *Sociology of Education*, 71(1): 54–67.
Thogersen, S. (2002). *A county of culture: twentieth-century China seen from the village schools of Zouping, Shandong.* Ann Arbor: The University of Michigan Press.
Tsang, M. (1994). Costs of education in China: issues of resource mobilization, equality, equity and efficiency. *Education Economics*, 2(3): 287–312.
Tsui, K. (1997). Economic reform and attainment in basic education in China. *The China Quarterly*, 49: 104–127.
Wei, X., Tsang, M., Xu, W., & Chen, L. (1999). Education and earnings in rural China. *Education Economics*, 7(2): 167–187.

White Paper. (2007). http://en.people.cn/90840/92283/92311/6285938.html, accessed 4/3/08.
Yan, Y. (1996). *The flow of gifts: reciprocity and social networks in a Chinese village.* Stanford: Stanford University Press.
Yan, Y. (2003). *Private life under socialism: love, intimacy, and family change in a Chinese village, 1949–1999.* Stanford: Stanford University Press.
Wacquant, L.J.D. (1989). Towards a reflexive sociology: a workshop with Pierre Bourdieu, *Sociological Theory*, 7(1): pp. 26–63.
Zellman, G. & Waterman, J. (1998). Understanding the Impact of parent school involvement on children's educational outcomes. *Journal of Educational Research*, 9(6): 370–380.
Zhang, Y. (2008). *Children's family background and teacher's educational expectation: comparative and international education society* (white paper). New York: Gansu Survey of Children and Families.

Index

Note: Page numbers with *f* indicate figures; those with *t* indicate tables.

academic help 99–100
academic information 93–7
Alexander, J.L. 48–49

banzhuren 6, 7, 40, 73, 93, 96, 110
bitterness, eating 57–8
Bourdieu, P. 7–8, 16–20; capital concept 16–17; habitus and field concepts 17–18, 33; rural parent social position and 28–9; social and cultural reproduction theory 16
Bowen, N. 13

capital concept (Bourdieu) 16–17
Carbonaro, W. J. 13
Chao, R. 14
Chi, J. 15, 48, 66
children: becoming dragon or phoenix 54–7; educational aspirations for 49–51, 49*f*; learning, work relationship and 78–81; repeating in school 70–1; responsibility, education as 63–71; role of, in China 67; walking out of rural areas 48–9
China: compulsory education in 23, 33; education system reform in 23–4; Law on the Protection of Minors 67; parental involvement in, perceptions of 14–16; role of child in 67; *suzhi* and modernization for education in 20–2
community support, as form of invisible parental involvement 14
cultural capital: linguistic and cultural competencies as 34; parental involvement as 18–20

Diamond, J. B. 14
Dufur, M. 13
Dumais, S. 63

eating bitterness 57–8
education: as child's responsibility 63–72; broadening horizons 58–9; family incomes and children's 15; mother's aspirations for achievement in 50, 59–60, 59–60*f*; opportunities for 100–2; for social mobility 51–4; valuing, changing dispositions toward 43–5
educational aspirations for children 49–51, 49*f*; educational achievement and 59–60, 59–60*f*
Entwisle, D.R. 48–49
Epstein, J. 12

Fan, X. 45
Fei, X. 42
field concept (Bourdieu) 17–18
Fong, V. 15

Gomez, K. 14
Greenhalgh, S. 20, 67
guanxi networks 92, 100–101

habitus concept (Bourdieu) 17–18; social class and 28
Hannum, E. 4*f*, 23
Hanson, M. 67
Hao, L. 23
Ho, E. 12
hopes and desires, parental: broaden horizons of children as 58–9; child becoming dragon or phoenix as 54–7; children walking out of rural areas as 48–9; eating bitterness and 57–8; for educational achievement 59–60, 59–60*f*; educational aspirations for children as 49–51, 49*f*; overview of 47–8; social mobility and 51–4

household chores: children's education and 15–16; learning environment and 83–4; parent educational expectations and 86–90
hukou system 8, 22–3, 103–4, 106, 113

importance of education 50–1
information gathering about education 94–6
intergenerational closure 13
invisible forms of parental involvement 12, 13–14,

Jaeger, M. 75

Kipnis, A. 15, 20, 21, 22, 48
Kinship relationship 67, 74, 92, 99–100

Lareau, A. 18–20, 33, 66, 101
Lawrence-Lightfoot, S. 33
learning environment, creating a good: financial worry and 81–2; household chores and 83–4, 86–90; learning materials in 76–8; overview of 75–6; parent sacrifice awareness and 84–6; work and children's learning relationship 78–81
learning materials, cost of 76–8
Lee, J.-S. 13
Lin, J. 15–16
linguistic/cultural competencies 34, 41

MacLeod, J. 49
migration for education: to cities 104–9; 109–112; literature 118; overview of 103–4; quality schools and 109–13; schooling transitions 104–6
minban teacher 6, 72
Murphy, R. 20, 21, 22, 46, 74

Naftali, O. 67

openness of students 41–2

Pang, C. 67
Parcel, T. 13
parental hopes and desires: broaden horizons of children as 58–9; child becoming dragon or phoenix as 54–7; children walking out of rural areas as 48–9; eating bitterness and 57–8; for educational achievement 59–60, 59–60*f*; educational aspirations for children as 49–51, 49*f*; overview of 47–8; social mobility and 51–4

parental involvement 11–12; invisible forms of 12, 13–14; as social and cultural capital 18–20; visible forms of 12–13
parental involvement in China, fieldwork on 3–7; ethnographic data 3; research site 3, 4*f*, 5; school/participant selection 5–7, 6*t*
parental involvement in rural children's schooling; *see also* rural parents: capital and 16–17; in China, perceptions of 14–16; Chinese education reform and 23–4; conceptions of, in China 14–16; conceptual framework for 25*f*; future research for 121–2; habitus and field 17–18; *hukou* and 22–3; invisible forms of 13–14; learning environment, creating good (*see* learning environment, creating a good); literature on 13–14; overview of 11–12; research site for 3–5, 4*f*; school and participants, selection of 5–7, 6*t*; as social/cultural capital 18–20; *suzhi* and 20–2; theoretical framework 7–8; visible forms of 12–13
parental social position 28–9
parent–child interactions, student achievement and 13
parent migration, reasons for 104; *see also* migration for education
parent sacrifice awareness 84–6
Park, A. 23
Pena, D. C. 14, 101
Putonghua 14–15; linguistic use of in schools 34, 41

Rao, N. 15, 48, 66
Reay, D. 18–20, 33
repeating in school 70–1
renkou suzhi 20
role models, encouragement and 52, 97–9
rural parental involvement, conceptual framework for 25*f*
rural parents; *see also* parental involvement in rural children's schooling: connecting, in schools 119–20; education officials thoughts of 1; family background and 29–34, 30–2*t*; hidden work of active (*see* learning environment, creating a good); hopes and desires (*see* hopes and desires, parental); linguistic/cultural competencies and 34; meaning of 27; openness and 41–2; rural area

constraints and 34; school resources and 34–6; social position and 28–9; *suzhi* and 27, 43; teacher interaction and 39–41; teaching quality and 36–9; valuing education and 43–5

Sayer, A. 18
Schneider, B. 103
scorpion-catching 80–1
social capital, parental involvement as 18–20
social class, habitus and 28
social mobility, education for 51–4
social position, rural parent 28–9
social support, as form of invisible parental involvement 14
socioeconomic status, parenting practices and 13–14
Stevenson, H. W. 15
Stigler, J. W. 15
student success: education as child's responsibility and 63–71; power and responsibility of learning 69–71; student's role in 62–71; teacher role in 71–3
support, family and friends: academic help 99–100; academic information 93–7; educational opportunities 100–2; overview of 91–3; role models, encouragement and 97–9
suzhi 11, 20–2, 34, 35, 43, 48, 116; of rural students 41; schooling and 43
Swanson, C. 103

teacher: interaction 39–41; role in 71–73, and student success
teaching quality 36–9

value of education 43–5
visible forms of parental involvement 12–13

to walk out, children 48–9
wenhua 1
wenming 20, 21, 29–30, 33
Willms, J. 12

Yan, Y. 67, 74, 92

Zhang, Y. 81
Zhao, Z. 21
Zhengxing Central Primary Schools 5, 47; descriptive statistics of 6*t*